Praise for *Do Eagles Just Wing It?*

"We are the authors of our own stories. The choices that we make shape our lives. How do you wish to change your life and what choices do you need to make to achieve your vision? If this is a question you ask yourself, then this book is for you."
David Gurteen, Founder and Director, Gurteen Knowledge Community

"Chip helps people better their lives and careers, and has great insight about people and their behaviors. That insight, and insights from his writing partners, has been translated into this book. Would you like to improve your outcomes both in business and in life? Then you should read *Do Eagles Just Wing It?*"
Herb Shear, CEO, GENCO ATC

"Look behind you, is anyone following? As leaders we can always ratchet it up a notch. We have no idea what we are capable of. This is a paint by number resource to make the leap and find out!"
Pat Riley, President/COO, Allen Tate Company

"Beyond answering the title's question, *Do Eagles Just Wing It*, this book prepares you to fly with eagles. Reading it is like having the content of a motivational lecture available for step-by-step use. You move through the process as if three coaches were sitting with you, giving you encouragement, and setting examples through singular stories, excellent exercises, and accurate assessments."
Elizabeth K. Fischer, Author of Mistakes I Made My First Five Years in Business (and How You Can Avoid Them), What's in It for Me? Marketing from the Customer's Point of View, and Mistakes I made Buying Advertising.

i

"Do Eagles Just Wing It" provides an intriguing and practical approach to guiding self-leadership in creating and delivering your personal "story" through focus and accountability. It is a great resource for personal development and growth."
Dave Thaeler, Senior Vice President, Haskell

"Insightful and real. An easy read with stories that everyone can relate to, and a clear reminder that success can only come from within."
Frank Anderson, President, RBW Logistics

"How do you know you are going in the right direction to achieving your wants, desires and goals? The authors have created an easy to follow process to help you understand the way to build a strategic plan for your life. Using these guidelines will help you make sure you do not just wing it.
The exercises are a great way to take the words off the pages and put them into action for lasting change."
Andy Smith, President & COO, Kenco Logistic Services, LLC

"I am so pleased to recommend *"Do Eagles Just Wing It."* As publisher of a regional business publication, I have the opportunity to visit and learn from business owners, managers and executives from a variety of business sectors. While many are very competent, they are all missing the critical input of an insightful "coach". The co-authors have done a great job taking what they use in their practice and putting it on the page. If you take the time to read the text and do the exercises, you can put the concepts to work in your life and work. You will not be disappointed."
John Galles, Publisher, Greater Charlotte Biz Magazine

"Only in stripping away the veneer of untruths we create for ourselves do we find the clarity and conviction to build toward something meaningful.

Within *Eagles*, the authors provide a practical, pragmatic framework from which to realize enduring personal transformation."
Jack Dwyer, Managing Partner, Black Diamond Transformation Group

"Feeling a loss of direction? Out of touch with your passion? Unsure of your next life adventure? Then get ready for a smorgasbord of insights and how to's that will help even the most confused souls regain a feeling of purpose and optimism. This isn't yet another cookie cutter self-help book, but a refreshingly written and presented guide to getting out of your chair and back into the stream of life."
Harvey Smith, CCMC,CPBA, CPVA, Head Coach, Carolina Business Coach

"This book uses stories and activities to engage any active reader who wants to move from the "Sky" to the "Nest" by developing clarity, focus, attention, and intention. The result should be to 1) build better relationships and 2) tell better stories. We can all benefit from such a nudge. Especially for those whose enthusiasm is dampened by career change or the recession, this book is a timely reminder of HOW to develop your brand. The authors' collaboration is a fine model for each of us, and I strongly encourage you to read their new book!"
Doug Gray, PCC, author of Passionate Action: 5 Steps to Creating Extraordinary Success in Life and Work

"If you're like me and learn better via metaphors and stories than from flowcharts and theory, *Do Eagles Just Wing It?* might just be the most appealing business book you'll read this year. The authors weave tried and true strategies with inspiration and aspiration sparking the reader's desire to soar higher than before."
Dee Bailey, CPCC, Transition Coach

"I enjoy books that are easy to read and leave some lasting impact on the way I think about things. This book is one that I have enjoyed. The three authors have told some great stories and put them into context. I am already thinking what I can do differently because of reading *Do Eagles Just Wing It?*"

Gary Mayfield, CEO, Kenco Logistic Services, LLC

DO EAGLES JUST WING IT?

SUSAN
NIELSEN

TRACY
LUNQUIST

CHIP
SCHOLZ

Copyright © 2011

Published in the United States by
Insight Publishing
707 West Main Street, Suite 5
Sevierville, TN 37862
800-989-7771
www.insightpublishing.com

ISBN - 978-1-60013-753-2

10 9 8 7 6 5 4 3 2 1

Table of Contents

Foreword

We wrote this book for two reasons. The first is to benefit you, the reader, through the creation of a relationship. Every time you pick up a book, you form a relationship with the author. As you turn the pages, you are either drawn further into that relationship, or you make the decision to end it. If you finish reading this book to the end, our hope is you will have benefited from that relationship.

The second, and perhaps more compelling reason for writing this book is to share some stories that may resonate with you, with the hope the stories make a difference in your story. Everyone has a story. From the time you are born, you create your story. Your parents, friends, business associates, life partners and children are all a part of your story.

While all the people in your life share in your story, they only see a moment or series of moments. You get to tell the story to some people and can shape it in any way you like. Others in your life hear your story from you and then observe how the story plays out. You are the only one who knows your whole story.

You are also the author of your story. You have a choice in how it comes out. While events may happen around you, you have the ultimate choice. Will you take the new job or stay in the old one? How will you react to friendship as well as the failure of friendship? How will you handle economic, political and social changes? What choices will you make that will change your life?

If you were attracted to this book, it may be because you have a desire for change. It could be a desire to do different things or to do things differently in your life or work. It might be a desire to be more efficient with your time, or more effective in your relationships. It may be the desire to move to the next level, whatever that means to you. In effect, you are changing your story. We are here to help you rewrite the chapters you choose.

In this book you will find a number of ideas, principles, and definitions that we, the authors, use in our life and work. Are we completely congruent with all the concepts in the book every day? No. Like you, we are each a work in progress.

The challenge for all of us is to be a little better every day. To live according to a vision and be a bit more purposeful every day. To make progress on achieving our goals every day. To be better in relationships with the people we encounter every day. To write the best story we can.

That is our challenge to you, the reader. Don't try to do everything in the book. Do one thing, change one behavior, and get good at it. Once you have made it a habit, do another one. Get good at it. Get in the habit of making and keeping promises to yourself. Little things do add up.

You may want to keep a journal or notepad handy as you read. There are a number of exercises and questions within these pages and you may find it useful to have one specific place to keep your thoughts and responses. There is a natural progression in the exercises, culminating in the Appendix at the end of the book. There you will find a suggested format for completing your Personal Strategic Plan.

Thank you for entering into this relationship with us. We appreciate the time you invest in considering the ideas in this book. Thank you for your willingness to throw away some of the things you know for sure and give yourself a chance for some new beliefs and new habits to take hold. Let us know how it works out. Two-way communication is important in a relationship! Our contact information is below, and we would love to hear from you.

Most of all, enjoy *Do Eagles Just Wing It?*

Tracy Lunquist: tracy@workingmagic.net
Susan Nielsen: susan@leaderscapes.com
Chip Scholz: chip@scholzandassociates.com

Introduction

By Joel Anderson

Chip Scholz has been my executive coach for the past several years. Chip and his writing partners have compiled the knowledge and practice I have learned during the time I have worked with Chip. He and his writing partners provide a great framework for understanding these principles. The book is an easy read. Putting the principles into practice is much more difficult.

I came to Chip as a successful executive with a successful track record. However, I wanted to take my performance to the highest level possible. I had "been there and done that" concerning operating a profitable, growing business. I now desired the capacity and ability to run a best-in-class business. To achieve that result, I had to become a best-in-class executive.

Great performance starts with great leaders, or "eagles" as the authors call them. My forty years in the workplace and over thirty-five years in varying levels of management followed by executive positions attests to that. After reading these pages and considering their impact on my life and career, I came to two conclusions:

My first and most obvious conclusion is that all leaders set examples, good and bad. To lead a high performance team you must always set a good example. Be purposeful, set solid goals and have a bedrock set of values.

My second, less obvious conclusion comes from working with a coach. You cannot get solutions from your home, your colleagues or your Board. They offer you opinions, recommendations, facts and conclusions, but only *you* can take the data and convert them into an action plan. And, to be candid, every one of those parties will provide advice from their viewpoint of you. What you must have to become a high performance executive is someone who knows you, understands your methods of excuse and avoidance, and holds you accountable to your vision.

Self-made, high-performance executives are the rare birds indeed, despite what the mirror might say to us. To provide our employees with world-class leadership, we all need someone in our lives to help us clear out the excuses, because our employees deserve the best we can offer. And that is what you will find in this book.

Joel is President and CEO of the International Warehouse Logistics Association in Chicago. He has more than 30 years' experience leading trade associations to higher levels of achievement. He may be reached at janderson@iwla.com.

"Though no one can go back and make a brand new start, anyone can start from now and make a brand new ending."

Carl Bard

Prologue: Eagles and Chickens

Once upon a time, on cool spring day, a man and his wife were out taking a walk around their farm when they came upon a baby eagle lying on the ground. The eagle was alive, but injured and alone. Knowing the bird was not likely to survive out of the nest, the farmer took off his jacket, wrapped the eagle in it, and took the eagle home.

The farmer wasn't really sure what to do with the eagle, so he put the bird in with the chickens. The chickens happily took in the little eagle as one of their own. The farmer was amazed at how quickly the eagle settled in, ambling around the pen, pecking at the ground and eating chicken feed. He even joined the chickens in the coop to sleep at night.

As the eagle grew, he started noticing he was different from the other chickens. The eagle's wings were larger and wider, and he was taller and stronger than they were. The other chickens had straight beaks, ideal for eating seed, but his curled over, and it was getting harder and harder to pick up seed when he pecked at the ground. Plus, the seed just wasn't all that satisfying. In addition, the other chickens didn't seem to have the perspective he did. He could see the farmer coming a mile away, whereas the other chickens didn't seem to notice the farmer until he was right there with them, tossing out seed. He tried not to worry about these things, but he noticed more and more that he didn't really fit in.

Then one day, he heard a strange but hauntingly familiar noise. He raised his head and looked to the sky, trying to pinpoint the source of the sound.

There they were. Two eagles flew overhead, soaring higher and higher into the sky. As he watched them fly, the eagle felt a spark of energy he had never felt before. He took a deep breath, and with great enthusiasm, started to run across the yard. Some of the chickens watched and darted away in confusion as he picked up speed. Others called out to him, screaming, "No! Don't do it! You're going to get hurt!" He thought for a second about stopping, but then, just a few feet from the picket fence, he spread his wings and flew!

*Up, up, up the eagle soared, flying for the first time, joining the eagles in the bright blue sky. He finally knew his true calling. **He was an eagle, not a chicken**. The chickens stared up at him, awestruck, filled with pride and joy, as if they had known it all along. And from that day forward, he lived the life of an eagle, never returning to the chicken coop.*

Are you an eagle in a chicken coop? Or maybe you feel like a chicken trying to figure out what's up with that funny looking guy with the white head and the sharp beak. As coaches, we have found most of our clients are more like eagles than like chickens, and once they leave the coop, they don't go back.

The Sky, The Ground, and The Nest

We'll be spending a good deal of time with eagles in this book, and so we've divided the book into three eagle-friendly sections—The Sky, The Ground, and The Nest. The Sky is about the big picture and the top-level considerations to be sorted out in order to live your best life. The Ground is about the specifics and details to be executed day to day. And The Nest is where we bring it all home. You'll see what we mean as you read. Should you choose to use this book for this purpose, we have also included tools and exercises to guide you through the process of creating a strategic plan for your life.

Within each section you'll find many stories we hope you will find both fun to read and thought provoking. The stories serve to illustrate ideas related to four basic building blocks we will revisit repeatedly: clarity, focus, attention, and intention. Let's look at each of those a bit more closely.

Building Block #1: Clarity

Have you ever tried to find something when you didn't know what you were looking for? Imagine yourself in your house or apartment, standing in the middle of a room looking for something without knowing what it is. It could be big or small, heavy or light, right in front of you or stashed away in a drawer for safekeeping. You may search and search, but to no avail. Why? Because you don't know what you are looking for.

Eagles know what they are looking for. It is hardwired in them. An eagle's eyes can spot an animal as small as a rabbit from two miles away.

It's a different thing that happens when you buy a new car, whether it's actually new or just new to you. Maybe you've never seen that particular car on the road before, or you have seen it, but in a different color or trim style from the one you bought. You may have thought there were only a few on the road, making your purchase unique. Inevitably, you drive the car off the lot only to find they are everywhere, in the same color and model you just bought. Why? That particular make, model and color of vehicle is in your mind's eye. It's in your awareness. Now it seems to be everywhere you look.

Clarity comes when you define, in no uncertain terms, what you really want to create in your life. It's where you are going, as well as your path to getting there. Remember, you can have just about anything, but you can't have everything. You have to determine which anythings you want. That's clarity. It clears the way for Building Block #2.

Building Block #2: Focus

Have you ever looked at an out of focus photograph? It's irritating, isn't it? In today's world of digital photography, you probably don't worry about blurry photos much anymore, as most cameras do the focus work for you. But every now and then, if you click that button too fast, you get a shot that is out of focus.

According to Merriam Webster's online dictionary, when something is "in focus" it "has or gives the proper sharpness of outline due to good focusing."[1] Good focus takes a concentration of attention and effort.

By definition, you can only focus on one thing at a time. You may have several things you give attention to, but technically, you focus on each one independently. That means you concentrate, attend to and expend effort on one task at a time, leaving one task to focus on another. A great example of this is driving and talking on a mobile phone at the same time.

Technically, if you are focusing on the conversation, there is no way to focus on driving, and vice versa. In reality, your attention shifts back and forth between the two all the time. You can't give the person on the phone your full attention and fully concentrate on your driving at the same time.

Eagles have tremendously sharp focus. While people can only see three colors, eagles see five. They can see through camouflage and pick out the sharpest details.

In your personal strategic plan, once you've clarified what you want, you'll choose areas of focus—those things you want to attend to in the short term to help you move toward attaining your wants. Your plan will provide focus for your most valuable resource: your time.

Building Block #3: Attention

It's not enough just to clarify what you want and focus on it. You must also pay attention, be aware, and see opportunities when they come around.

The words "soar" and "eagle" go together well. Eagles are known to soar for hours at a time, covering lots of ground.   Golden eagles in Wyoming may cover as much as 100 miles in a day looking for their prey. While they are soaring, they are constantly paying attention to their environment.

Paying attention is about ensuring you're in the right place doing the right things to move you forward on your success journey. It's about noticing when you find yourself flying off to random places, attending to distractions rather than to what is truly important to you. It's also about constantly evaluating your clarity and focus to ensure they are still valid. As time passes and you have new experiences, your wants may shift or change.

Additionally, sometimes distractions show up at the party dressed like opportunities. If you are paying attention, you'll be able to assess each distraction and evaluate it against your current statements of clarity and focus, and make conscious, informed decisions about whether it's an opportunity to pursue now or in the future.

Building Block #4: Intention

At this stage, you've gained *clarity* about your wants, have *focus* on what's most important, and are paying *attention* for new opportunities. Now it's time for action. *Intention* means acting with meaning, significance and purpose.

Being "on purpose" helps you make the changes you want to make to be your best possible "you". Change is neither easy nor quick. Consider the molting process of an eagle. It takes almost half a year to replace its 7,000 feathers, starting with the head and working downward. It's a process, not an event, and uncomfortable (perhaps even a little ugly) while it's happening.

In the same manner, successful leaders implement change with deliberate thought and planning for the good of the entire organization, leading by example and avoiding hasty or disruptive decisions. Great leaders also recognize that change is challenging under the best of circumstances, and support the affected people through the pain of the change.

Being "on purpose" is harder than it sounds. Have you ever set out at the beginning of your day committed to work on something specific and come to the end of the day without touching it? Working in an intentional manner takes practice. Think about what you were doing today before you picked up this book. Were you intentionally engaged in your activities? Were you giving each activity your all? Or were you just going through the motions?

Working with intention implies giving everything you do significance—everything has meaning. It's a powerful way to live. If you acted more often with intention—with awareness of purpose and significance, what would be different or possible in your business? Your relationships? Your health? Or your free time?

If we are truly honest with ourselves, we know we spend a lot of time and energy unintentionally. If you can learn to harness even a little more of that energy and apply it with intention, you can change your results in big ways.

Strategic Learning

A plan for living "on purpose"—a personal strategic plan—is the outcome of strategic thinking about your life. Strategic thinking is a learning process. Your personal strategic plan should not be an end in itself, but rather the beginning of a process of implementing, learning, revising and moving ahead—a process of personal learning and achievement.

The process of learning is often uncomfortable. If you've ever learned to ride a bike, play a musical instrument, or drive a vehicle, you've experienced the frustration, anxiety and general discomfort of learning something new and developing new habits. You also know the thrill of success when you finally pedal your way around the block, perform well at a recital, or pass your driving test.

Because your life plan will continually change as you discover and incorporate new opportunities, it's a good idea to write out your plan simply and measurably to ensure you truly achieve your goals. Keep your plan out in the open, exposed to others, visible and sometimes a bit messy, *not stashed away neatly in a drawer*. It may need to be rearranged, corrected, scribbled on or torn up and rewritten many times. You may need to share a little, or a lot of it, with people whose help you need to implement it. This may be very daunting and uncomfortable at first, since most of us have at least one negative experience when we've opened ourselves up to others only to be rejected by them.

There will be people in your life—friends, family, colleagues and others—who will try to hold you back from attaining greater levels of success. It is not typically malicious, and they may not even do it consciously; in fact, in their minds they are doing it because they care about you. They will warn you not to take risks because they don't want you to be hurt. Remember the eagle's chicken family and how they frantically warned him not to fly?

It would be ideal to know that your family, friends and all the people around you are all in your corner, picking you up when you're down, dusting you off and shoving you back into the ring, and then cheering you on to victory. But realistically, you can't always count on that happening. Clarity about your plan, focus on your desired outcomes, attention to your goals, and intention to succeed will help you work through those challenges and come out on top.

Looking Skyward

Are you ready to soar with the eagles? Then let's explore The Sky, using our building blocks—clarity, focus, attention, intention—to consider those top level, big-picture components. When you are a strategic learner, the sky is the limit!

Part One: The Sky

"Celebrate your success and stand strong when adversity hits, for when the storm clouds come in, the eagles soar while other birds take cover." –
Unknown

Spirit in The Sky

If eagles could talk about flying, they might say some of the same things wise old guys who fly antique biplanes say. Wise old pilots know airplanes fly more efficiently if they work with the air instead of against it. By understanding the air, and how different factors like heat, humidity, clouds, wind and so forth affect it, a pilot, or an eagle, can choose the path and altitude that will provide the smoothest flight, and can even discover the thermals—pockets of warm air moving up—that will carry them effortlessly to breathtaking heights.

In The Sky we'll explore how cruising thermals, working with current conditions, choosing and holding a good attitude, and using affirmations can help you gain altitude.

Clarity: Cruising Thermals

If you have spent any time watching eagles soar, you probably noticed that they constantly look for thermals. A thermal is a rising column of air created by warming of the earth. The sun warms the ground and the air warms above it. Warm air rises and expands until it cools and falls back to lower altitudes.

Air constantly changes. Humidity increases and decreases. Temperature goes up and down. Wind speed and direction vary, sometimes moment by moment. Eagles must assess and respond to these changing conditions constantly in order to choose the behavior that harmonizes best with the movement of the air.

Like the air, changes in our lives bring new choices that create uncertainty. The more choices we have, the more uncertain we may become. Because uncertainty is uncomfortable, change usually causes resistance. But, what looks like resistance is often a lack of clarity. Clarity becomes the thermal that lifts you up and lets you soar without flapping. When you know what you want, choices are easier and you are less likely to get caught up in distractions that look like opportunities.

Dreaming Is More Than Just Having Your Head in the Clouds

It was 2:00 on a sunny Thursday afternoon in July. The class gathered in the conference room, anxiously awaiting the arrival of the two leaders. Some of the participants chatted and shared stories. Susan sat quietly and nervously, unsure of what she had gotten herself into. Finally, the leaders arrived. After a short introduction, they announced the first exercise called My Dream Is. The participants were asked to greet everyone in the room one by one by introducing themselves and sharing their dreams.

"Dreams?" Susan thought to herself. "What do they mean by dreams?" Susan tried to raise her hand to ask a question, but the group was already in motion. Everyone seemed to understand the exercise except her. As the first person approached, Susan felt anxious and sweaty in discomfort. Just then, she overheard the conversations next to her. "Hello, my name is Jennifer," the person said. "And my dream is to go up in a hot air balloon." "Hello, my name is Sonya. And my dream is to spend a month in Australia."

"A-ha!" Susan thought with excitement. "I get it. What are my dreams? What do I actually want?" Coming up blank, she decided she'd just "steal" everyone else's ideas and get through the exercise. The first person smiled and asked, "Do you want to go first?" "Sure!" Susan said with delight. "My name is Susan and my dream is to go up in a hot air balloon." "Oh, that's a good one! My name is Sharon and my dream is to sing in a band."

And so it continued. "Hello, my name is Susan, and my dream is to...
sing in a band."
travel to Australia for a month."
take a cruise."
write a book."

At the end of the day, on her drive home, Susan vowed to get her own dreams. Over the course of the day she realized she had spent all her time making sure other people got what they wanted, and somewhere along the way had lost sight of what she really wanted.

Whether you are like Susan and have no idea what your wants are, or like the others in the class who knew exactly what they wanted, it is critical at this stage for you to recognize and claim your wants. To "want" means "to feel a need or desire for." Wants are what you crave, what you wish for. Wants generally indicate something you need to feel complete, but are currently lacking. A want may also be something you are inclined to correct or change or need release from.

Our minds are filled with desires of all kinds: tangible, intangible, short-range, long-range, major, minor, general, specific, modest, outrageous. In many ways, our modern society has placed such value on "being an adult" and "having our feet on the ground" that like Susan, we find it difficult to uncover these desires and find the freedom to express them to anyone, even ourselves.

Your wants are personal and unique to you, and they need not make sense to anyone but you. Some of your wants may seem completely illogical. Others may just seem way out of reach right now.

Each of your wants is like a thermal, providing warmth, lift and motivation when you need it.

Thinking about what you want may cause some frustration at first. You may wonder, especially for some of the more immediately doable things, why you haven't achieved them already. Pay attention to the ways you censor your own wants. Notice the "judgments" you have about your own wants, as well as any "shoulds" which come to the surface, but be careful not to let them derail your list making efforts.

Your want list is the foundation for the rest of your plan. It's important to give this part of the process the time and attention it requires. Use the exercises on the next few pages to brainstorm and uncover your deepest needs and wants. And remember, though you'll move on to developing the next components of your plan, you can always add, subtract or modify the wants on your list. Your list will change as you change.

All your wants, no matter how big or small, are valid and valuable. Your want list is a sanctuary of possibilities. All your desires are welcome here. It is from defining what you truly want that your vision will be born.

Exercise: The WANT Generator

To use the WANT Generator, associate each of the words listed below on the left, with each of the life areas listed below on the right, then write the desires that flash in your mind onto your Want List. Be sure to include everything.

Wanting Words	Life Areas
HAVE	FAMILY
DO	FINANCIAL
ACHIEVE	SOCIAL
BE/BECOME	PHYSICAL
GO/VISIT	MENTAL
SEE/DISCOVER	SPIRITUAL
KNOW/LEARN	PROFESSIONAL/CAREER
FEEL	
CREATE	
OWN	
BUILD	
GIVE	

Exercise: Let Me Ask You This

Still having trouble getting your dreams on paper? Here are some questions that may help you find your way:

1. What do you want your self-image to be?
2. What kind of qualities would you want people to say you have developed?
3. What books do you want to read?
4. What subjects do you want to learn about?
5. What plays, shows or cultural events do you want to see? Where? With whom?
6. How often do you want to get together with friends? To do what?
7. What five people do you want to meet in your lifetime?
8. What hobbies do you want to have?
9. What kinds of civic, charitable activities or organizations do you want to be involved in?
10. What do you want your appearance /physical fitness to be?
11. What kind of physical activities or sports do you want to participate in?
12. How do you want to feel? What do you want your health to be in the future?
13. When do you plan to be out of debt? How much would you like to have in the bank?
14. In what kinds of things would you like to invest?
15. In what kind of house would you like to live?
16. Where would you like to be in five years? Ten years? Twenty years?
17. How can you be a top performer in your current career? Your future career?

18. What changes do you want to make to your home?
19. What things do you want to do for your family?
20. Where do you want to go with your family on day trips? On extended vacations?
21. Where would you like to go a second time?
22. What would you like your ethical/spiritual life to be like?
23. What are your religious roots, and do they still resonate? What, if anything, do you want to do about it?
24. What would you like to learn more about in the way of spirituality?
25. What things do you want to own? What car do you want to drive? What else?

A Final Word About Your Wants

It's easy to get caught up in judgment about the things we want. Perhaps you have just a few wants on your list, or maybe there are pages of them. You may have a very practical list or an entirely fantastical list. Whatever your wants, don't forget, the key word is YOUR. Please take an extra second to be sure the items on your list are truly yours.

With your want list started, you have the foundation to make some choices, consider current conditions, and decide where to place your focus.

Focus: Current Conditions

The sun is out. It's a beautiful day. Big white puffy clouds push past each other against a summer blue sky. There are clouds in all kinds of shapes and sizes, and each cloud shifts and moves as it travels, pushed by the wind. You are ten years old, and you and your friends decide to take a break from your busy play schedule to lie down in the grass, looking up and calling out the shapes of the clouds.

It's probably been a long time since you last took the time to lie on the ground and name the shapes you see in the clouds. And we suspect you haven't looked to the clouds lately to help you focus.

Pilots, however, do just that. Before each flight, pilots check out the current conditions, making sure the type and size of today's clouds are conducive to a successful flight. Even large airliners change flight patterns based on clouds, winds, storms and other weather patterns. Focus on current conditions is essential to a safe and productive flight.

Your next step in this process, then, is to consider "current conditions" so that you have a productive life. We'll call this focusing on your purpose.

There is a story told by motivational speakers quite often about the meaning of purpose. Perhaps you've heard it. When told by a gifted speaker, there is a general sense of reverence around the telling, and the audience is supposed to get a lump in their throat or even a bit misty. It's a good story, but we think the motivational speakers may be missing the point.

The story is about Sir Christopher Wren. In 1668 he was commissioned with the task of rebuilding St. Paul's Cathedral after a great fire heavily damaged it in 1666. Rebuilding it took more than thirty years, and Sir Christopher was there, watching over the construction.

In 1671, Sir Christopher Wren was walking through the worksite when he came across three bricklayers doing their work. One was hunched over, working slowly, one was working a bit faster, and the third was standing and working fast.

He walked up to the first man and asked, "What are you doing?"

The first man thought for a moment and answered: "I am making a living."

Wren moved on to the second man and asked him the same question. The man looked at the priest and replied, "I am working to provide for my family."

Finally, he asked the third bricklayer what he was doing. He replied, "I am building a cathedral for people to worship and glorify God!"

The typical takeaway is that the third one was purpose driven, and the only one who got it right. It was why he worked the hardest and was the most successful of the group. His answer is the one meant to put a lump in your throat as you think about living your purpose. Living within your purpose is certainly important, and it is powerful to imagine a grand purpose when your work is like bricklaying—difficult, repetitive, heavy yet precise, and exhausting—but is "building a cathedral to the glory of God" the only grand purpose?

In his own way, each bricklayer got it right for himself. Each worked toward a grand purpose, the one that made the most sense for him personally. Even more fundamentally, each bricklayer defined success for himself. All three had taken the time to visualize what it meant to be successful in what they were doing.

How about what was not said? The "why" didn't include the "what." Not one of the bricklayers said they were doing their job because they liked laying bricks. The "what" was necessary, but not necessarily important. They focused on what success looked like to them, and worked toward it.

Similarly, when a pilot takes to the sky, she may be flying for a variety of reasons. Perhaps she is taking a load of passengers or cargo from one location to another. She could be on a solo flight, practicing or honing her skills in acrobatic flying. Or she could be logging hours toward becoming an instructor. Each has a different "why" in focus; that is, they all have a unique, personal view of success that goes beyond simply flying the plane.

With that in mind, we propose the following definition of success, which we will use throughout the rest of this book:

"Focusing on the why, success is self-defined, dynamic, and touches all areas of our lives."

Just like your want list, how you define success is your choice. It is of utmost importance to be clear about your definition.

Exercise: Defining Personal Success

Here is an exercise to help you begin to put together your own definition of success. Think about what success means to you, personally. Think about all the moving pieces of your life. Then take out a sheet of paper and write down a list of the things that define success for you. Don't write a paragraph for each, just a couple of words. Write as many as you can or feel you should. Then go back and rank the list in order of importance to you.

Now, take a look at what you wrote. What do you notice? Did you find that you wrote down more than one item? Did you list material items, intangibles, or both? Were there more of one than another?

Do any of the items you wrote have an end point? In other words, do you ever "get there?" If one of your items was to be a great parent, a great spouse, or just be happy, is there a time when you achieve your success and quit? Is there a time when you become happy and stay happy the rest of your life? Or must you continue to work on being happy? Are there specific ways you will know when you attain success?

Let's take this process one step further.

Consider a big puffy cloud. It isn't just one big round blob, but a combination of many different size cells, all mixed together, moving and changing size as conditions change. Let's use that visual to help define success more clearly. Below is a diagram of a cloud made up of various size circles—your very own cloud.

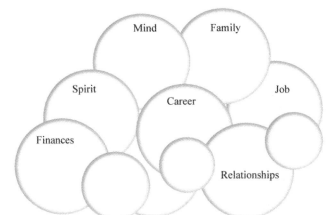

Now build your own cloud diagram. Use the headings listed below or feel free to add others you think are important. Think about the relative importance of each area of your life, and make the cells for the most important areas larger than other parts of your cloud.

Consider these questions as you design each cell:

Mind: How would you rate your level of mental development? Do you have a regular reading program? Do you regularly challenge yourself to solve problems in a more creative manner? Are you curious? Do you consistently learn new things?

Body: What is your level of satisfaction with your physical being? How is your health? Do you take care of yourself? Get enough sleep? Eat well? Exercise?

Spirit: How would you rate the strength of your belief structure? Do you have a written set of beliefs that guide your actions? Do you regularly reexamine your beliefs? Are you part of a spiritual community? Do you want to be?

Finances: Do you have some kind of budget or financial plan? How satisfied are you with your financial picture? Do you have a savings plan? How about insurance? Are you preparing for retirement?

Job: Are you satisfied with your current position or job? Do you find it stimulating and satisfying? Do you get some sort of satisfaction from doing a good job?

Career: How does your job fit into your overall career plan? Do you have a career plan? Are you ahead of or behind where you pictured yourself at this stage in your career plan? Where do you want your career to go, and how do you rate your chances of getting there?

Family: How satisfied are you with your family life? How are your family relationships? Do you maintain regular contact with those family members close to you? Do you do things for them, and they for you? Do you count on them, and they on you?

Relationships: How satisfied are you with relationships outside your family? Do you have a wide circle of acquaintances and a close circle of friends? Can they count on you and you on them?

Community: How do you participate in the world? Do you support a cause? Do you give money or volunteer time to a charity? Are you aware of what is happening in the government at the local, state, national or international level? Do you vote? Are you a member of one or more clubs or organizations? Do you want to be?

Next, shade in each cell with the level of satisfaction you have in each area of your life. For instance, if you are seventy percent satisfied with the number, nature, and depth of your relationships, color in seventy percent of that cell from the bottom up.

When you have finished filling in each cell, take a look at what you created. Did you have any cells not colored at all? How about items under sixty percent? Perhaps these are areas in your life in which you are either unsatisfied or dissatisfied. Do you know the difference?

Unsatisfied means you haven't paid much attention to that particular area, or it is an area you would like to grow in. Dissatisfied means you are unhappy or actively upset about that particular area. Unsatisfied means you are hungry, dissatisfied means you had the meal and it is causing indigestion. Unsatisfied causes yearning and anticipation. Dissatisfied causes pain and frustration.

Which is it for you? More importantly, do you want to do something about it?

Like the pilot, as you assess the "current conditions" of your life you can make choices about your path. Similarly, eagles always assess current conditions in flight. They stay very aware of the winds of change, navigating through and around the clouds. It's important for you to regularly take stock, reconnect with or revise your definition of success, and consider your wants and options. Do you want to stay on the track you've been following, or is it time to change your flight path? As you consider your definition of success, where do you need to focus your attention?

The areas you choose to pay attention to will depend on your attitude.

Attention: Attitude

Each of us has a basic set of beliefs which encompass the "things we know for sure." They have developed over a lifetime. We hold these basic beliefs about ourselves, other people and the world. These beliefs are our attitudes.

Our beliefs are our attitudes, our attitudes are our behaviors.

Our belief system is the underpinning of our set of attitudes. Attitudes drive behaviors. Behaviors are the observable actions which define us to other people. Behaviors are the outward expression of the things we know for sure. We behave in ways shaped by our attitudes. We rarely behave in a way contrary to our basic beliefs. Some of the things you know for sure may help you and some may hurt you, but your beliefs make you the person you are.

Attitudes are our self-talk.

Attitudes may also be defined as the things you tell yourself. Your attitudes drive the conscious and subconscious self-talk that governs how you act or react in a given situation. We have hundreds of these conversations with ourselves every day. Some of the conversations are memorable and part of our decision-making or problem solving abilities. Some don't make it to the level of conscious thought, but are still active in our minds.

How good are you at remembering names?

This isn't a rhetorical question. Answer honestly. How good are you at remembering names? In most groups asked that question, more than seventy percent raise their hands and admit having difficulty remembering names. Some proclaim, almost proudly, "Oh! I'm TERRIBLE at it!"

There are two components to the answer. The first is attitudinal, the second behavioral. Whether you say you are good or bad at remembering names, your answer reveals two basic attitudes.

The first attitude your answer reveals is about the conversations you have with yourself. No matter whether you said you were good or bad at remembering names, your words describe the internal conversation you have about remembering names. When you heard the question, you had an immediate, silent, internal conversation, which led to the answer you gave.

Suppose you said you were bad at remembering names. Here is the external and internal conversation you might have when meeting someone for the first time. This is the behavioral and attitudinal outcome of your conversation.

You, external conversation: "Hi, my name is Bill, nice to meet you. What's your name?"

Them: "My name is Gary."

You, external conversation: "It's a pleasure to meet you!"

You, internal conversation: "I'm not going to remember your name anyway, why should I care what it is?"

You may not have that conversation consciously, but the effect is the same, isn't it? When you say you are bad at remembering names, it is a self-limiting belief statement.

Your actions and reactions were based on long held and supported beliefs. The beliefs were formed or developed at some time during your life. You had some experience leading to your belief. Similar experiences over the years led you to greater conviction in that belief.

The other attitude displayed is how you view others. In other words, what do we think about when meeting someone for the first time?

As humans, we are very "I-centric" organisms, and that's okay! Most people generally tend to focus on themselves. It's how we thrive and survive. When it comes to talking to others, we want to tell our stories. We think about what we want from the other person. It might be reflected in our concern for how we look, whether our hair looks good or whether we have lettuce stuck in our teeth. If we are in sales, we size up the other person, think about how he or she might help us, and what they can do for us. We are all self-focused.

If we want to change the way we remember names (or anything else), we have to change our beliefs about others and our ability to remember names. We have to first change the self-talk that got us there. We also need to change our focus from ourselves to the other person.

The first step is to start telling yourself that you are good at remembering names. Use an affirmation to help you to change your beliefs about names. (Don't know what an affirmation is or how to use one? Don't worry. It's coming up in just a few pages.)

The second step is to put the focus on the other person and not on you. This is the behavioral piece mentioned above. The new behavior is to ask questions. If you ask questions and really listen to the responses, an amazing thing happens. You get answers! Asking really good questions gets you really good answers most of the time. Aren't you always amazed at what people tell you if you just take a moment to ask a question and then listen to the answer?

Don't be afraid! Ask!

Chip was waiting to get his hair cut. A young woman bounced into the hair salon, and went over to the corner of the room to grab a magazine. As she backed out of the corner, she ran into a big cabinet full of hair care products and knocked about half the bottles and jars over.

She looked up, and to the rest of the waiting room she said, "I am so clumsy."

What do you think her basic beliefs are? Of course it's obvious. She believes she's clumsy. She tells herself she is every time she does something she sees as clumsy. She knows it for sure. It's a basic attitude about herself and her place in the world.

Being the kind of person Chip is, he asked her, "Well, how long have you known you were clumsy?"

Remember, if you ask a question, most people will answer you. She did.

"When I was five years old, I was standing on a desk and my shoes were untied. I tripped over my shoelaces and fell off the desk."

"How did you know you were clumsy? How did you know it just wasn't unfortunate or that you just did something dumb?" Chip asked.

"Because everybody told me I was clumsy," she said. "The teacher, the other kids, even the janitor who had to clean up after me."

Chip then asked, "What other times have you felt clumsy in your life?" She recounted several other times when she knew she was clumsy. There was the time she tripped and hit the bumper of her car and had to get stitches in the back of her head. There was the time she caught her heel on the carpet and rolled down the stairs in her prom dress to meet her date. There were plenty of reinforcements for her major belief.

Her name is Gina.

She had come to North Carolina to marry a young man from the area. She was from New Jersey, and concerned about marrying into a Southern family. In fact, her future family wasn't so pleased their little boy was marrying a Yankee girl. (If you've spent time in the South, you might understand.)

Once you know their back story, it's very difficult to forget someone. Funny, though, isn't it? Chip never told Gina his name or his story. It wasn't important for him to talk about himself. What mattered was to learn Gina's story, which she was more than willing to tell. It's all about the attitude you have that drives your behavior when you meet someone new. Chip remembers Gina's name because he remembers Gina's story. And it's a pretty good bet Gina remembers Chip, even though she doesn't know his name.

Thinking differently about remembering names, or about any other attitude you hold, will help you devise different ways of behaving. And when you do things differently, you'll get different outcomes, eventually creating a shift in your beliefs. Start by simply noticing that the "thing you know for sure" is not an objective fact, but an attitude.

Attitude is so important in flying, that airplanes have an instrument called an "attitude indicator" which the pilot checks periodically to make sure the plane stays oriented the right way. When you first learn to fly, holding a consistent attitude in your airplane is hard work—you find yourself wandering from it and needing to make corrections. With practice, it gets easier and more automatic. The same thing is true in developing your personal attitudes. At first, you'll need to give it a lot of attention and make a lot of adjustments, but after a while, it will become natural. In the next section, we'll look at how affirmations can help you set and act on your intentions, change your behaviors, and develop attitudes to help you succeed.

Intention: Affirmations to Gain Altitude

Most people now know Al Franken as a United States Senator. However, at one time he was a comedian who appeared on *Saturday Night Live*. He played a character named Stuart Smalley, and the bit he did on *SNL* was called "Daily Affirmations with Stuart Smalley." His tag line, you may remember, was "I'm good enough, I'm smart enough, and doggone it, people like me!"

Smalley's tag line was his list of affirmations. And he did a great job of satirizing affirmations! In each of our coaching practices, we've dealt with the hangover of Senator Franken's skit. Affirmations have taken a real beating. There seems to be a high degree of skepticism around using affirmations as a tool for personal improvement.

Yet few tools are better for changing your mind in a positive direction than affirmations. Affirmations change the story we tell ourselves. By changing the story, we change the way we think. When we change the way we think, we change what we do and we change our behaviors.

Changing your behaviors starts with changing your thoughts. It's a progression:

- If you change the way you think about things, the things you think about will change.
- When your thoughts change, you start to ask different questions of yourself and others.

- When you change your questions, you start to get different answers, different information.
- When you get different information, you can make different choices.
- When you make different choices, you do different things.
- When the things you do change, you get different outcomes.
- If you've been intentional about defining your outcomes, your ability to get what you want increases.

And isn't that the point?

The Brain Science of Attitudes

Depending on your behavioral style and attention span, this next section may be a bit theoretical for you. We are going to get into a bit of science, but if you can hang with it, you may find it helpful in understanding how beliefs are formed in the first place.

In the past fifteen years we have learned more about the way our brains function than ever before, primarily because we have better scanning technology than we've ever had. Before the mid-1990s or so, we had no medically safe way to look at a living brain in action, so our research was limited to cadaver brains. Unfortunately, dead brain tissue doesn't tell us much about how brains actually function.

But in the mid-1990s, we gained the technology to view the brain "in vivo," or alive and functioning. We could track the electric signals as they pulsed through our brains, and we could better understand the mechanism of our conscious and subconscious. As a result, we found many of the things we thought we knew for sure just weren't true.

For the first time we could see the brain "light up" when certain stimuli were presented. We could watch decisions being made. Not only could we see the form, we could watch the function. Here is a small portion of what we learned with one caveat: research continues at a rapid pace, and while we know the following at the time of this writing, we are learning more and refining our understanding every day. In twenty years, what is true now could be different again, but this is our best current science.

The basic building blocks of our nervous system and brains are cells called neurons. The typical human brain has between 25 million and 30 million neurons at birth. These neurons have tiny arms extending from the cells called dendrites. Dendrites form connections that allow us to store up our experiences.

Every time we have an experience or learn something, the dendrites match up with each other and form a synaptic connection. These synaptic connections form our memories by creating intricate neural networks and pathways. The dendrites don't permanently bond, but instead create mini-thunderstorms between them, which produce a powerful, but not permanent, electronic connection.

By the time we are three years old we have about 15,000 synaptic connections. Some of these contain hundreds of thousands of neurons, depending on the intensity of the experience. Some contain fewer. By the time we are seventeen years old we only have 3,000 synaptic connections. Where did they go?

Well, those connections that are repeated or reinforced become bigger. The smaller, secondary connections fold in on themselves to form larger primary connections more easily accessed. The largest of these connections form your beliefs, or the things you know for sure—your attitudes.

Changing Actions by Changing Belief

All you have to do to act differently is to believe different things. Sounds simple, doesn't it? Didn't we just spend the last several paragraphs explaining how our beliefs get hard wired?

It isn't simple at all. It takes hard work and intention to change your beliefs. Perhaps it will help if Chip tells some of his story here:

Chip was an athlete in his younger years, but time and good living had crept up and done what time always seems to do. He was a bit thicker around the middle, not as strong and flexible, and his health numbers told a sad story. Each year seemed to bring a new medication, and each year his numbers seemed to get a little bit worse.

His father died at fifty-two of cancer, and his mother wasn't far behind, dying at fifty-five. Both had smoked and lived a typical lifestyle for their generation. Chip was only twenty-seven when his father died and thirty when his mother passed. In a way, he felt his parents' deaths were his own death sentence, and he would be lucky to outlive them. So for years, he didn't pay attention to his own health and for the most part ate what he wanted and exercised intermittently. When given the choice between a healthy alternative and a riskier one, he tended to pass on the healthy one.

Eventually, Chip developed Type II Diabetes. At first he was able to treat it with diet and exercise, but over the course of fifteen years, he now needed two insulin shots a day and eleven different medications to deal with diabetic problems. Without changes, Chip would eventually succumb to one of those problems. His story already seemed to be written, and the ending clear.

At 53, Chip had already outlived his father. To him, it was kind of a shock. He never really considered living longer than 52! And now he actually faced living with all the choices he had made up to that point. Yikes!

He decided to act. He chose to change his story, and perhaps its ending. At the time, he was fortunate to be working with a coach. With his coach, he set some clear and specific goals, including:

Weigh 245 pounds (the least he had weighed as an adult)
Have an Hba1c (long term measure of blood glucose) of less than 7.0%
Have a total cholesterol level of 175 and an HDL level of 45

When he set his goals, his coach asked him to develop an affirmation to support his new behaviors. Because Chip thought he should humor his coach, he thought of some. He then embarked on a journey to change his story and improve his health.

After several months, nothing much had changed. Chip was clearly struggling, and he felt frustrated. His behaviors didn't seem to be changing much. As he wrestled to reach his goals, he expressed his frustration.

His coach asked, "What affirmations are you using?"

Chip was an avid fan of Saturday Night Live and remembered all too well the Daily Affirmations skit. "You know, I just don't get affirmations," he told his coach. "All that stuff is just a bunch of hoopla created by the people who wear hemp dresses and believe in power crystals."

"Wow," said the coach. "I guess you have a bunch of work to do in changing that story, don't you?"

As his coach explained what affirmations really mean and how Chip could use them in making changes in his life, the lights started coming on, albeit dimly. Reluctantly, Chip agreed to give affirmations a try.

Three years later, Chip still works to be healthier. However, his goal setting and affirmations led him to a vegan diet, a physically active lifestyle, and the belief he can truly live much longer than either of his parents. He is off insulin, has his cholesterol and blood sugars under control for the first time in fifteen years and feels better than ever. Chip credits affirmations as the fuel that fired his change engine. He changed his story by changing his mind.

Fueling the Fire: Affirmations

Affirmations are new stories we tell ourselves in order to change our minds in positive ways. They are simple statements which, when repeated over and over, train our brain in a new belief system. To understand how it works, let's go back and revisit the brain.

Our brain has a conscious side and a subconscious side. Our conscious brain processes at the rate of about 2,000 bits per second. Our subconscious brain processes at 4,500,000,000 bits per second.

Our conscious brain understands concepts like time. We plan and set our goals there. We consciously and systematically create the synaptic connections that allow us to learn in our conscious brain.

Most of the processing happens in our subconscious brain, but with a difference. It is the residence of our memories. It is the part that takes what we read and compares it to other things we know and either accepts what we know, modifies it, or rejects it. Our presenting stories—the things we know for sure—reside in our subconscious.

Talking to the subconscious brain is a lot like talking to a three year old. If you have small children or grandchildren, you know exactly what that means. There is no tomorrow. Everything is excruciatingly present. Kids live in the now. There is a great Walt Disney World® commercial that features a kid in his room thinking about their trip to the Magic Kingdom®, and his line is "I'm too 'cited to sleep!" What they don't tell you is that he probably said it three months before the trip!

This is a vast oversimplification of the actual brain processes, but illustrates clearly how we find ways of doing amazing things. Or stop before we even start.

An affirmation is one of the little mind tricks we can use to change our outcomes. They are positive statements, within your capacity to believe, written in the first person singular and present tense. The statement expresses your desired state, and is written *as if* you have already achieved (or returned to) that state. An affirmation reminds you, in times of confusion, stress or doubt, of that which you know to be true at other times. It is how you keep going, even in the face of long odds.

An Affirmation

✔ States what <u>will</u> be true, not what <u>won't</u> be true

✔ Is expressed in first person, present tense, *as if* it were already true

✔ Is emotionally compelling and exciting to you

In reality and truly in effect, you are creating a powerful statement for your subconscious. Remembering an earlier statement, your subconscious only understands what is, not what isn't. Therefore "losing weight" or "quitting smoking" has no resonance. It is only when discussing what will be—weighing 195 pounds, running a marathon with a healthy set of lungs— that we start to "get it." An easy way to ensure your affirmation is expressed in first person and present tense is to start it with "I am a person who..." or "I love it when I..." As you get good at creating them, you may be able to start simply with "I."

Here are some examples of affirmation statements:

- I am a person who is healthy. (This is one of Chip's.)
- I love it when I honor my children.
- I am a person who enjoys the company of others.
- I love it when I am impeccable with my word.
- I am a person who is grateful every day.
- I love it when I trust others.
- I am a person who sells well by giving value to my clients.

Take a moment to think of two or three affirmations of your own. Imagine something you are having trouble accomplishing. Think of a goal you want to accomplish. Then write an affirmation to support that goal.

Once you have created your affirmations, use them. Do this by creating a habit, flooding your mind with the affirmations you have made for yourself. To do this, grab three index cards or sticky notes, and write your affirmations on each one. Put one of the cards where you will see it in the morning (on the mirror you use to get ready for the day), one where you will see it in the middle of the day (on your car's instrument panel if you go out for lunch), and one where you will see it at the end of the day.

Now let's learn a way to lock affirmations in and make them really powerful. This technique takes advantage of the three most powerful learning modalities for adults: sight, sound, and feel.

Take a moment, and reconnect with a specific instance when you were really on fire. It could be the time you accomplished something you had been working on for a long time. It could be the moment when you won a sporting contest, or gave a great speech and got a standing ovation. It could be the birth of a child. Simply a special moment, one filled with emotion, summoned by just closing your eyes and returning to it.

As you connect again with the moment, ask yourself the following questions, and be very specific about the answers:

What do you see around you? What is the scene like? Who are the people with you and around you? What colors stick out in your mind?

What do you hear around you? What sounds are in the background? What are other people saying to you and about you? What are you saying about yourself?

What do you feel? Take a moment and focus on the emotion. When you are fully back in the moment and feeling the emotion, ask yourself:

- Where in your body do you feel it?
- What shape is it?
- If the feeling had a color, what would it be?
- What temperature is it?
- How does it feel if you touch it? What is the texture?

If you were able to describe the emotion in physical terms, have you ever been able to describe it that way before? Was it surprising to do so? Assuming the emotion was a positive one, was it something you would like to experience and feel again? By reconnecting in this way, you can.

Finally, tie the emotion to the affirmation you are working on to build up its poignancy. In this way, you build your motivation. The words 'motivation' and 'emotion' both trace back to the Latin word *movere*, meaning "to move." Both emotion and motivation move you to achieve your goals. Emotion fuels motivation, motivation drives achievement, achievement fuels emotion, and so on. The fire is fueled, and you're ready for takeoff.

Phugoids

Al Haynes knows way too much about phugoids.
There is a reason you should, too.

*On the afternoon of July 19, 1989, United Airlines
Flight 232 took off from Denver Stapleton airport,
bound for Chicago. Captain Al Haynes manned the
controls, and looking at the weather and flight plan,
anticipated no problems.*

*At 3:16 in the afternoon, about an hour after
takeoff, the sound of a loud explosion came from the
back of the plane. The frame of the aircraft
shuddered and lurched to the right. Haynes's first
thought was that the plane was breaking up, and he
would die in a massive fireball. But then, after a few
deafening seconds of metal gnashing against metal,
the quiet returned and the plane kept flying.*

*Captain Haynes and his First Officer, William
Records, scanned the instruments for some kind of
indication that something was wrong. The pilots
noticed the number two engine, the middle engine
in the rear of the plane, had stopped running. Such
a failure can be dangerous, but it's rarely
catastrophic, since the DC-10 has two additional
engines, one on each wing. Haynes pulled out the
pilot manual and started going through the engine-
failure checklist.*

*While Haynes worked through the engine failure
checklist, Records flew the plane. After a moment or
two of working with the controls, Records turned
and said something no pilot ever wants to hear:
"Al, I can't control the airplane."*

What could trigger such a complete loss of control? Haynes noticed the pressure in all three hydraulic control lines was plummeting towards zero. The hydraulic systems control the airplane. In the DC-10 there were three redundant lines in case pressure was lost. Never before had a plane lost all three without a catastrophic crash.

Engineers later calculated the odds of losing all three systems to be more than a billion to one. Yet it had happened. It was simply unthinkable. Being unthinkable, no procedure had ever been developed for flying a plane with no hydraulic systems and no tail engine.

Haynes, a senior pilot with thousands of hours in the air, had an idea. The DC-10 had an engine on each wing, and those were working fine. He could control those without hydraulics. Each engine could be controlled independently by a technique called differential thrust. Haynes decided to try using it to control the airplane.

There was little time to lose. The bank was becoming severe enough to put the plane into a death spiral. Haynes advanced the throttle on one engine and slowed the other. At first nothing happened. But then, ever so slowly, the right wing began to level itself. The plane now flew in a straight line. The desperate idea had worked.

Just as the flight crew started to gain a little confidence, the plane began to pitch up and down. This is known as a phugoid pattern. Phugoid refers to the repeated exchange of altitude for airspeed. A plane begins to lose airspeed. The nose points down, gravity takes over and the plane gains speed. As speed increases, so does lift. As lift increases, the nose lifts until the speed and the lift are lost. The cycle then repeats.

Under normal conditions, phugoids are easy to control. However, with loss of hydraulics, the phugoids would continue as the plane plummeted inexorably down. To control the phugoids, Haynes realized when the nose tilted down and the air speed build up, he should increase power, allowing the two remaining engines to bring up the nose. Because the engines of the DC-10 are set below the wings, an increase in engine throttle will cause the plane to pitch up. In other words, he needed to accelerate on the downhill and brake on the uphill.[2]

Haynes used Clarity to see the outcome, executed with Focus, paid Attention to actions and reactions, and moved the throttles in an Intentional manner. By doing so he saved the plane from falling out of the sky.

Phugoids happen to us all the time. Very rarely do we have level flight throughout our lives. We have short and long term ups and downs in our families and our careers. When things happen to us in flight, we may not have much control over the circumstances. We do, however, have a great deal of control over our actions and how they affect our outcomes.

Think more about Captain Haynes's story. He was well-trained and had a well-trained crew. He had a plan, but not everything went according to the plan. That is the nature of plans. Because Haynes had thought through the plan, he could come up with possible solutions. If we prepare well enough, work hard enough and think, we have a better than average chance of making it to the ground in one piece. Sometimes the answers are counter-intuitive. By keeping a level head and an open mind, while flying the airplane you have and never giving up, you can survive even the billion-to-one odds.

As we will see in the next section, we develop our plans on the ground. We think through what we want, and create plans to get those outcomes. And when we hit the inevitable phugoid, we are ready.

Part Two:
The Ground

"The whole wide earth is the eagle's way."

– Euripides

Clarity: Your Vision

Eagles know their priorities. They must find food, connect to a mate, build a nest, feed their chicks, and migrate if the climate is not suitable for year-round living. Eagles also have amazing vision. Their eyes are about the same size as a human's, and *four times* as sharp as the best human eye. Interestingly, they also have two "foveae," or centers of focus, that allow them to see forward and to the side at the same time. In the case of the eagle, its remarkable vision serves its priorities. For you, developing a remarkable vision will help you clarify your priorities.

When you created your want list, you opened your mind to many possibilities. Now you're ready to take your work to the next level and craft a statement or expression of your vision. Your vision provides the foundation for day-to-day decisions and energizes actions toward a better future. It answers the question, "What will my life look like in the future?" It's your personal "call to action." It's a statement of potential and a description of who or what you want to become.

For some, creating a vision is easy. Perhaps you've always had a clear picture of your life.

Brenda was one of those people. From a very early age, Brenda knew she would go to college, get a PhD, and become a college professor. Along the way, she would connect with a man who shared her vision, marry and have children. She would live in a nice home in the midwest, work at a small to mid-size university that focused on education without the pressure of constant research, and be a mom. They'd camp and eventually build a cabin on a lake.

When the kids were grown and they had saved enough money, they'd sell the house, live in the cabin in the summer, and travel around the world.

For others, creating a really long-term vision is terrifying. When John left for college, he didn't quite know what he was going to do with his life, but thought a major in Business Administration should be general enough to cover many bases. Over the years, John put together a solid resume and had many challenging and rewarding roles. He bought a new, larger house in a recently developed area of town he had his eye on for the past couple of years. When John tries to envision his future, he has a tough time seeing past a year or two. His focus is on the short term.

Do you see yourself in Brenda or John? Perhaps both?

Whether your vision is for your entire life, like Brenda, or for shorter periods of time, like John, what really matters is to choose or set a timeframe that is realistic, meaningful and inspiring to you. Set the vision out too far and you may not be motivated to take action or stay the course. Set the vision too close and you may get discouraged by the prospect of failure. Either way, if your vision sounds nice but doesn't motivate you, you won't do anything.

You can use your Want List (created in Part One) to help you draft your vision. Consider:

As you review your wants, are there any common or recurring themes?

In general, what do the items on your want list tell you about you?

What wants can you really see yourself achieving?

 What is in your heart to do, no kidding? What would be too cool for words?

Is there a single want or a few wants most critical to you right now?

Are there any wants you could achieve in the short term if you focused on them?

What wants are truly important for you to achieve?

Which one is most important?

Who are you when your most important wants are satisfied?

Are there any items on your list that, if left undone, would leave you feeling unfinished and unfulfilled? When you close your eyes and see your future, what is different from today?

Go into detail with your vision. What are you like in your future? What are you doing? With whom? Who is around or with you? Where are you? How does it look? How does it smell? How do you feel? What color is it? What do you hear, see and touch?

Get involved with the details of your vision and then write down the answers to the questions. Writing your answers—the very experience of writing them—will change how you experience the answers themselves. Choose the words and format that work for you. You may have a nice, neat vision statement or you may have a simple list of words that evoke your vision. You could create your vision in pictures, colors, even scents. What is most important is to be clear about your vision. Use descriptions that bring you clarity and motivation.

Remember, your vision needs to be something you connect to, so make it uniquely yours. It doesn't have to be eloquent or sound or look impressive to other people. This is your time to be all about you! Be sure to write your vision in the present tense, as if you have it already. A vision statement is, first and foremost, an affirmation!

Your vision is the cornerstone for the rest of your Strategic Life Plan, so take your time and work through this exercise until you have a vision that rocks *you*.

Focus: Your Values

To value something means to assign it worth, merit or importance. It implies some intrinsic excellence or desirability. Value is that quality of anything which renders it desirable or useful. Core values are often viewed as the more spiritual qualities of mind—ethics, character or morality.

On the surface and intellectually, the concept of values is easy to understand. Most people say, at least, that they know and live by a set of core values. However, when given a blank sheet of paper and asked to list their core values, very few people can do it without much thought and consideration. They may claim they have a "gut feel" for their values, or know them "in general." Some may live according to a standard set of principles, but can't articulate them easily.

Achievement	Discipline	Harmony	Money	Solitude
Acknowledgement	Dominance	Health	Morality	Spirituality
Adventure	Earnings	Honesty	Obedience	Stability
Altruism	Education	Independence	Order	Status
Artistry	Environment	Initiative	Peace	Success
Autonomy	Excellence	Innovation	Philosophy	Sustainability
Beauty	Experience	Intellect	Pleasure	Taste
Candor	Experimentation	Insight	Politeness	Tenacity
Challenge	Exploration	Integrity	Power	Thrill
Comfort	Fame	Intimacy	Precision	Touch
Compassion	Family	Inventiveness	Principles	Valor
Connection	Fitness	Justice	Recognition	Variety
Consistency	Freedom	Knowledge	Respect	Wealth
Contribution	Friends	Leadership	Risk Taking	Wellness
Creativity	Frugality	Learning	Safety	Winning
Curiosity	Grace	Leisure	Security	Wisdom
Danger	Happiness	Love	Sensitivity	
Daring	Hard Work	Mastery	Service	

When it comes to creating the life you want to have, values play a key role. This is not the place to just "wing it." Values are the basis for everything we do. They are the basis for our motivations, interests, attitudes and desires. Our values give us a sense of direction and purpose.

Achieving success, but doing it out of alignment with your values, will not be nearly as satisfying as it could be. The media is full of stories today about people who achieve great levels of success by setting professional ethics and personal values aside. Perhaps you've heard the saying "cheaters never win, and winners never cheat." In truth, sometimes cheaters do win the game at hand, but they never really "win" because they know at their core they had to cheat to do it.

Values are highly personal and develop through a long and sometimes subtle process based on life experiences. For example, after working in a passive-aggressive work environment, where feedback is sugar coated, you may develop the value of candor. If you watched a parent work long and hard his entire career for the same company and be rewarded consistently for his efforts, you might highly value loyalty.

Understanding your values has a very practical application. You perform better when your thoughts, feelings, emotions, goals and values are in alignment.

So how do you go about identifying your values?
In the table on the previous page are several words representing values. Review the list and circle the ones that hold high importance to you. Feel free to add words to the list as they come to you.

Next, review the words you circled, as well as those you added to the list. From these, choose your top eight values. Write each value, as well as a description of what that value means—your definition of how you live this value. Think of it as how the value looks in action. For example, "candor" may be described as "I am direct and tell the truth to my friends, family and colleagues. I do this in a way that is honest, objective, unassuming, and not accusatory. I ask them to do the same for me. I am accepting without being defensive."

Finally, from your list of eight, choose the top four or five that truly represent your CORE values—the ones you would never compromise—the values you wouldn't trade for *anything*.

Once you have your final list, consider the implications of the values you've chosen on your life as it is today, as well as on the vision you've created for your future. Where do your actions and behaviors of today align with your core values? Where are they out of alignment? What do you need to start doing, stop doing, or continue doing to be in alignment with your values right now? Looking to your future, what implications do your core values have on your vision? Are they in alignment with your vision? Do they change or shift your vision? If so, how?

You may find your values have a distinct impact on your vision. That was the case for Jennifer, an HR Manager at a large manufacturing firm. When she first crafted her vision, she envisioned herself working her way up to the executive ranks in Human Resources. The work she put in on developing her values, however, revealed core values of service, achievement and learning. Her

51

HR position was quite transactional in nature, with some opportunity to coach and mentor other leaders and associates, but those opportunities were sporadic at best. She spent most of her time putting out fires, investigating issues, ensuring policy adherence, and taking care of paperwork. She rethought her vision, choosing a career path in operations instead, where she could directly lead and manage a team, with emphasis on helping them learn, grow and achieve results. She also set her sights on finding a nonprofit organization for which she could volunteer and utilize her HR skills.

The key is to use your values to determine what is truly important, and then ensure your vision is in alignment. Together, your vision and values provide a foundation of clarity and focus, setting you up for development of your critical success factors.

A Note about Congruence

Greater congruence is one of the major outcomes of a successful coaching relationship. In this context, congruence means to develop a rapport with yourself by being consistent with yourself and those around you. Others see you as sincere with a degree of certainty, and they are drawn to you because of it.

Without congruence, it's very difficult to believe in yourself. In a recent *Parade Magazine* "Personality Parade" piece, Tina Fey said, "The beauty of self-doubt is that you vacillate between extreme egomania and feeling like 'I'm a fraud.'" While we don't know if Tina is congruent, her statement would suggest she is not.[3]

By taking the time to create a vibrant and exciting vision for the future, as well as a behaviorally defined set of values, the process of congruence begins. Developing congruent critical success factors and SMART WAY goals (more on SMART WAY goals coming up in a few pages) continues the process. Living according to your vision and values by achieving your goals develops congruence.

For example, let's take a look at Chip's coaching career. Chip is successful by his own and by most people's standards, and at this time in his life, he now feels congruent. It wasn't always that way.

Chip spent most of his career working for big companies. He was quick with a smile, able to string sentences together and make sense, and did enough homework to ensure he could talk the right talk at the right time. When he was laid off, he wasn't sure what he was going to do, but decided to hang a shingle and learn about personal development.

Chip sold his pants off and soon the business was coming in. In fact, he started to do quite well. However, when it came time for clients to continue working with Chip and do more business, they did not. And when it came time for clients to refer him to other potential clients, they also did not.

Outwardly, Chip was the picture of success. He said all the right words, nodding and smiling at the appropriate times, but it just didn't work, because inwardly, Chip felt like a fraud. Someone once told Chip the definition of an expert is someone two chapters ahead in the reading. Chip took that to heart, and it caused him to feel incredibly incongruent.

He preached use of affirmations, but didn't use them. He didn't read much or broadly. He didn't spend money on his own development even though he wanted clients to spend money on theirs— preferably with him. He didn't have a strategic plan, marketing plan or any other kind of plan for his business, or for his life. Worse, after some great initial results, his business revenues started falling instead of growing.

That incongruence translated into internal turmoil. Externally, he couldn't let his clients or anyone else know what a fraud he thought he was, so he became cocky and arrogant. If anyone crossed him, he would become defensive, critical and difficult.

Chip had a choice, as we all do.

He hired a coach. He hired someone to facilitate him through his own strategic plan. He went through his initial training course one more time along with all the newbies. He set goals and used affirmations to achieve his goals. He began reading, initially a book each month, which eventually developed into a book or two per week. And a funny thing happened. Somewhere along the way, he became congruent.

If you ask him, Chip won't be able to tell you the point at which he transitioned. It might have been when he started getting referrals. It might have been when he started getting calls asking him to speak and share his secrets. It might have been when he was able to sleep through the night without waking in a cold sweat from the strain of faking it.

As you enter into the tactical stage of your plan, the Critical Success Factors and Goals, you might be tempted to skip a step. It's important to resist that temptation. When you've done the work, you won't feel like an impostor.

Attention: Critical Success Factors

There are roughly seventy items that must be addressed when getting ready to fly a Cessna 172 airplane before you even start the engine. There are almost twenty-five more steps in starting the engine, making ready to let off the brake and begin moving. Needless to say, a larger or more complex aircraft involves even more steps. As an airplane passenger, would you want the pilot to do all that from memory and just hope he doesn't skip a step? I bet not.

Some students at a university had been building autonomous airplanes to fly in student competitions over the past few years, without great success in the endeavor. They did okay, but they really didn't seem to have a competitive edge over the other teams.

Since this kind of project naturally attracts many engineering students, most teams fall under their school's College of Engineering. In the particular case of this team, their project had not attracted a pilot—a person with real-life flying experience who understood how airplanes differ from cars or boats.

When a pilot finally joined the team, he suggested right away that the team develop checklists. Pilots use a checklist to make sure they don't skip any of the important steps in preparing for and conducting a flight. Every good pilot, no matter how many thousands of hours they've flown, how familiar they are with the airplane, or how short or simple the flight, uses a checklist every single time.

By developing a series of checklists for their autonomous airplane, the students improved the safety and efficiency of their test flights. That meant fewer crashes, more time in the air, and ultimately, better performance at the competition.

In your life plan, Critical Success Factors are like the headers on your checklist. Once you decide on your destination (your vision and wants) and what kind of airplane you'll use to get there (your values), you'll need a checklist to make sure your flight is safe and efficient. CSFs are the categories in which you consider the specific items you should examine and address. On an airplane checklist, those headers include "Preflight Inspection," "Engine Start," and "Before Takeoff."

If your destination included financial well-being, for example, your CSFs might include getting out of debt, buying life insurance, or maintaining a profitable portfolio of investments. As you can see, each of these factors is more specific than the high-level want of "financial well-being," but is not as specific as a goal such as "retire my student loan from First Bank of Moneytown by December 31, 2015" might be.

Remember Jennifer? She decided to change her vision from HR Executive to operations leader when she considered her core values. She established four critical success factors to achieve her overall vision, including this shift in career focus. CSF #1: Transition to Operations. CSF #2: Financial Planning. CSF #3: Family. CSF #4: Personal Wellness.

When Chip decided to change his health, he set critical success factors such as lose weight, reduce cholesterol, and use affirmations. Chip identified several CSFs to help him achieve congruence including hiring a coach, writing a strategic plan, reading, and truly becoming an expert in his field.

In short, CSFs give you an outline for your checklist. It's an inventory of items that require your attention in order to achieve your vision. Once you have your CSFs in place, you're ready to break down your plan into specific goals.

Intention: Goal Setting the SMART WAY

Strategic planning isn't something you do from beginning to end. It's something you do from top to bottom. You start with the big stuff—vision, mission, values—and drill down to the specifics. Achieving goals happens the same way, just on a narrower scale. The Goal Achieving System, or GAS, when thoughtfully applied to your goals, becomes the fuel source to power your efforts and get what you want.

Before you can achieve a goal, you must define it. Otherwise, how will you know you have succeeded? In order to set a goal, and not simply dream, create a fantasy, or just have one of those "gee, I really ought to ___ " items on your list, construct it the SMART WAY.

SPECIFIC
MEASURABLE
ATTAINABLE
REALISTICALLY HIGH
TARGET DATE

WRITTEN
ALIGNED
YOURS

Your goal should be **SPECIFIC.** What, exactly, do you intend to do? Describe your desired outcome as clearly as you can. When you set specific goals, you tend to get specific results. When you set unclear goals, you will have a hard time visualizing yourself achieving them. Let's look at a very common example of an unclear goal: "I want to lose weight."

Okay, how much? How soon? If you step on your scale every day for a couple of weeks, I can promise you there'll be one morning the number is smaller than it was yesterday. Congratulations! You've lost weight! Check that one off! Hmm. Maybe not. By contrast, a specific weight-related goal is "weigh 185 pounds by December 31." This goal comprises a specific objective with a specific timeframe to achieve it, and on December 31, you will know with perfect certainty whether or not you were successful.

It should also be **MEASURABLE.** Measurable goals are important in two ways. First, measurable goals allow you to set interim "waypoints" while navigating toward your ultimate goal. Those waypoints give you the ability to schedule actions on several dates leading up to your goal. Second, not every goal you set will be 100% accomplished. However, you did make progress, didn't you? When you can measure the progress, you can take your wins and celebrate your successes, and even redefine your goal with a higher or lower bar based on your experience.

It must be **ATTAINABLE.** Very few things are impossible, but some are so unlikely as to make their pursuit demoralizing. You may be absolutely determined to become a Formula 1™ race car driver, but if you are a lightly built woman learning to drive for the first time at age 60, the best attitude in the world probably isn't going to get you there. If you set unattainable goals, the frustration of failure will really hurt your self-confidence.

That is so not the point! So rather than setting an impossibly aggressive goal, make it **REALISTICALLY HIGH.** Maybe Formula 1™ is too great a stretch, but stock car racing in a local contest isn't. Find the most ambitious version of your dream that is attainable, and set your sights there. Marianne Williamson said, "Your playing small does not serve the world." If it is within the capacity of your mind and body, make it happen.

Give yourself a **TARGET DATE.** The best-defined goal with no deadline is still just a dream.

Get it **WRITTEN DOWN.** The "power of the pen" is no mere cliché. Writing makes it real. Putting your goal in writing creates a performance contract with yourself. It forces you to clarify your thoughts and make a commitment to realize your dreams. Once written down, sharing it is easy. Most goals will take some help to accomplish, so why not have them available to share in written form?

You will most readily achieve the goals **ALIGNED** with your life strategy. Every goal exists in the context of the rest of your life. Checking each goal for alignment with your vision, values and mission helps you decide how important it is to you, and whether this is the right moment to start pursuing it. Be sure your goals align as well. If one goal is financial security, and the other is to take forty-eight weeks of vacation each year, that could create some problems.

Most importantly, make sure the goal is truly **YOURS.** Human beings are keenly skilled at achieving other people's goals. We work hard to make our bosses look good. We respond to the needs expressed by our kids, our spouses, our parents. We take pride in "being there" when our friends need us. But we frequently forget or postpone the things that matter most to us. If you have trouble achieving a goal that appears personal, such as streamlining your spending or becoming more physically fit, ask yourself who you're really doing it for. If the answer doesn't look back at you in the mirror every morning, it's no surprise you're having a rough time of it.

Step on the GAS

Once you have your goal defined in the SMART WAY, it's time to find out if you're serious. There's a good chance you are, if you've gotten this far, but GAS is only useful as a fuel when it's fired up. You'll need some raw passion to ignite the GAS, and that passion comes from one simple question:

So what?

Suppose you achieve this goal—so what? What will it do for you? How will it feel? Write down your answers or say them out loud. Then ask yourself why you said what you said. Then ask yourself why you said that. Keep asking, until you've peeled back at least five layers of "why." Asking this question taps into our "possibility thinking" patterns. In other words, it lets us discover all the wonderful implications beneath the surface of achieving the goal—joy, satisfaction, excitement, pride.

After you've gone five layers of "why" into "so what if I achieve this goal?" do the exercise again, asking yourself, "so what if I *don't* achieve this goal?" By asking the question from this different angle, you will tap into your "necessity thinking" pattern. It explores the undesirable, potentially ugly and frightening elements of failure to achieve the goal. Although they may not be very comfortable to contemplate, those too can be very motivating.

Why is this exercise important, you ask? Tracy did this with a group of women using a fairly innocuous goal: saving up to purchase a new refrigerator. The first "so what?" was simply about wanting a shiny new appliance. But as Tracy started chipping away with "why?" she felt a mood shift in the room. The sense of accomplishment from saving rather than taking on debt. The pride of having a beautiful kitchen. The frustration of the balky performance of the current fridge and the worry about a leak or an unexpected failure. The raw fear of unwittingly serving spoiled food to the family.

These responses washed into the room on waves of intense emotion. If a group of businesswomen can get that riled up over a refrigerator, what's bubbling below your surface about a major life goal you've been contemplating, maybe for years?

As you can see, the "why" exploration is essential to the GAS process. Please do not skip this step! It will make the difference between achieving your goal and wasting your precious time. Once you've completed the "So what?" exercise, you should have one or more motivators that pass the "goose bump" test. In other words, thinking about the reasons you need to achieve this goal should give you goose bumps. If it doesn't, odds are this goal isn't as important to you as you think.

If your reasons fail the goose bump test, stop! Going forward from here is probably a waste of time. Choose a goal with more power to inspire you, rather than getting a few steps down the road with this one and abandoning it at the first distraction. False starts and loose ends severely drain your energy and self-esteem. They feed the monsters in your head, the ones that say you never finish anything or that you "can't." Of course you can, and you do, and you have, and you will. But only if the outcome really matters to you.

Fitting Your Goals into Your Life

GAS is a high-octane fuel, but it won't take you very far if you haven't taken the time to plan the route. An old, oft-quoted parable goes something like, "If you don't know where you are going, all roads tend to lead there."

Ask yourself, "If this is so important to me, why isn't it already done?" and then put your answers into one of seven areas of goal setting opportunity. This will help you discover the steps you need to take to achieve your goal, both the obvious and the not-so-obvious. The seven areas of goal setting opportunity are: **Time, Treasure, Talent, Manpower, Machinery, Providence, and Stupidity.**

Time. Perhaps the most common excuse for not achieving a goal is lack of time. We say, "Oh, I'll get to that eventually," or "I'm just too busy to pursue that dream." Consider your priorities, attitudes and other commitments. How will you make the time to pursue this goal? What energy management skills and motivators can you apply? How will you overcome your time limitations and fit this goal into the rest of your life? What is a realistic schedule and who can help hold you accountable to stick to it? Ask yourself, "What do I need to start doing to achieve the goal? What do I need to STOP doing to give me the time to achieve the goal?"

Treasure. "I can't afford it" is another popular excuse. "Afford" is a funny word. We use it whenever we don't want to buy something, regardless of our real reasons. Achieving a goal means making a commitment of all kinds of resources, and money may be one of them. What can you do with the resources you have right now? How can you make the most of your available treasure and get "the biggest bang for your buck?" Do you have to buy something outright, or can you rent, borrow, repurpose, scavenge, salvage or creatively finance? Can you "do it yourself" to save money on a product or service related to your goal? Is it worth trading time for money or vice-versa?

Talent. This refers to *your* talent—meaning the skills, capabilities, attitudes and values you bring to the party. What can you bring to bear to ensure your success? What external resources do you need to develop any missing abilities? What areas do you need to learn about? If you have a health goal, for example, do you know everything you need to know about diet, exercise or nutrition?

Manpower. This refers to the other people who influence your ability to achieve your goal. Who is likely to help? Who is likely to hinder? How do your own attitudes and beliefs about those other people match up to objective reality, and what bearing might that have on your goal achievement process? Where will you find the people who can help you? What do you want them to do once you find them?

Machinery. Machinery can be any inanimate object whose mechanical cooperation is required to succeed in your quest. What tools do you need? What talents do you possess in using those tools? Will you need to learn new skills, such as a new computer program or the use of an unfamiliar machine to achieve your goal? Who can help you? How will you respond to the setback if something breaks?

Providence. Previously known as "Acts of God," before political correctness, this refers to the random events that propel you unexpectedly and blissfully forward on your journey. Do you believe in magic? Miracles? Prayer? The Law of Attraction? How will you apply those beliefs to this process? How will you respond to something unimaginably wonderful happening? Specifically, how will you apply that happy accident to your process and remain focused to see your goal through?

Stupidity. Made you smile, didn't it? This is the opposite of providence—the random event, often, but not always, perpetrated by another person or people—that throws a massive monkey wrench into the works and sets you back. How will you respond to something unimaginably terrible happening? How do you remain focused to see your goal through? Keep in mind, the most vicious and skillful saboteur you will ever face in goal planning is yourself. Negative self-talk and self-limiting beliefs will do incalculable damage to your process if you let them. So don't let them!

Once you have completed your analysis and considered each of these seven key areas, you'll have a clear picture of what it takes to achieve your goal. Next, translate the information you've collected into a plan of action. Think in terms of concrete actions and the behaviors that flow from the actions. Outline the steps required and what resources you will need to take them.

Since the issues that came up in the different areas will probably overlap a bit and are not really oriented toward the time or order of steps in your goal achievement process, you may find it helpful to write your action steps on small pieces of paper or sticky notes you can rearrange as you discover dependencies or prerequisites.

Once you have a series of action steps defined, determine what steps, if any, can be delegated or shared with others. A spouse, parent, child, friend, employee or coworker may be able and willing to help, so ask! There's no need to travel the path of goal achievement alone. The magic marriage of support and accountability can make wonderful things happen.

Having defined and delegated all your action steps, you're now ready to put them into your calendar. What's the next step and when will you take it? Make the commitment in writing and stick to it.

Your Intentional Goal Setting process is nearly complete. Now is a good time for a reality check. As you look at your action steps in your calendar alongside everything else, does the plan look reasonable? Do the steps add up to the whole goal being achieved? Do your steps meet the SMART WAY criteria of your original goal? Is your original target date still appropriate?

Make any adjustments or corrections now, and be sure to revisit your plan regularly to make sure it still passes this reality check. Revise your target date if necessary and reward yourself for completing this critical first step in goal achievement by writing some affirmations related to your goal.

One last word about SMART WAY goals. Not all your goals will easily or neatly fit into this format. Is "being a better parent/manager/speaker/leader" a

SMART WAY goal? Probably not. Is it still a worthy goal? Probably so. Is that okay? Absolutely! We all need one or two "becoming" goals. Even if the goal itself doesn't meet the SMART WAY format, applying the SMART WAY discipline in your planning of it will help you achieve it. Being specific in the seven steps often leads to greater clarity about the goal.

Affirmations, Once Again

You already know from reading Part One of this book that affirmations represent a critical piece of your success puzzle. It's so critical, in fact, that we're bringing it up again.

It stands to reason you'll want to apply the power of affirmations to your goal achievement process. Strong affirmations around your goal keep it clear in your mind, help you stay focused, bring your attention back to the goal, and reinforce your intention to achieve it.

Remember to state your affirmation positively, in the first person and in the present tense. Imagine, as vividly as you can, how it will feel to achieve your goal. Devote as much time as you need to find the right words to express that feeling, or if you prefer, find or create pictures or even music to serve as your affirmations.

Whatever form your affirmation takes, keep it in several conspicuous locations so you'll come across it several times each day. If you've expressed it in words, say the words aloud frequently. If it's a picture, make several copies and keep them near your desk, on your computer, on the fridge and any other places you'll see it regularly.

Feel the fear (or pain or doubt) and do it anyway! Achieving goals is not always easy—sometimes downright daunting. Only you can decide what you are willing to do to achieve a goal. The clearer you are on what you want, why you want it, and what you are willing to endure to make it happen, the more likely you will be to succeed.

Going Up

For eagles, the sky and the ground are busy places, where clarity, focus, attention and intention are all critical and require quick thinking. And like people, eagles need to spend a good bit of time in both of these active spaces—up in the sky examining the big picture, enjoying the view, and seeking out the next opportunity, as well as down on the ground where the practical needs of life like food, water, and nest-building materials can be found. All this activity is so important that you could find yourself tempted to spend all your time out in the active spaces of life. But those who function at maximum capacity in the sky and on the ground have taken the lesson of the eagle and built a nice big sturdy nest. The nest serves as a sanctuary where eagles (and people) can rest, reflect, and rejuvenate.

Eagles make their nests in the highest available tree, positioning themselves dozens to hundreds of feet above the ground dwellers and nicely halfway between the ground and the sky. In our nest, we can explore the ways we get motivated and stay organized to make the best use of our time on the ground and in the sky.

Part Three: The Nest

"Eagles come in all shapes and sizes, but you will recognize them chiefly by their attitudes."
— *E.F. Schumacher*

Clarity: Bringing it Home

Have you heard of Jesse Owens, the fastest man alive? Jesse died in 1980, but his story has been woven into common lore and is even still taught to school children. Consider for a moment what he did that was so special.

Owens took first place and the gold medal in the 100-yard dash at the 1936 Olympic Games in Berlin, Germany. Many have run that race faster in the years since, but Jesse's achievement was so special because of the context. Germany was recovering from World War I. In the aftermath of losing the war, the German people had lost their national pride, their economy was far from healthy, and the nation needed a reason to smile.

Enter Adolph Hitler. A rising leader in Germany, he told the people they should be proud of their heritage and have hope for the future. He brought runaway inflation under control, offered structure and discipline to the masses, and engineered his "master race" of humans.

By 1936, Germany had survived and was thriving, and Hitler wanted to showcase his new Germany all to the people of the world. He sought to control the games—to win every event he could—and no race was more important than the 100-yard dash. Hitler would prove his people were the fastest and strongest in the world.

But along came Jesse, an African-American with four gold medals in the games, including, most importantly, the gold medal in the 100-yard dash. He won the race by one-tenth of a second, edging out the second place finisher and setting a world record in the process. In short, he embarrassed Hitler on his home field.

Coming home after the games he was given a hero's welcome and showered with gifts. His picture appeared on the coveted front of the Wheaties® cereal box. In those days, when someone was given a ticker tape parade, money was thrown into the honoree's car. At the end of the parade in Jesse's honor in New York, over $10,000 had been thrown into his car.

Do you know who came in second?

If you answered that it was a German, you would be wrong. If you answered "Who cares?" you would be giving one common answer, adopting a not-entirely-healthy American cultural belief that winning is everything.

The real answer? Another African-American. His name was Ralph Metcalfe. He was participating in his second Olympics. If Jesse had not run that day, Ralph would have tied the world record, won the race, won the gold medal, seen his own face on the Wheaties® box and enjoyed a ticker tape parade worth $10,000.

Since this was Ralph's second and final Olympics, coming in second could have been a devastating blow. It wasn't, as we will see, because of a simple and complex understanding—the power of purpose.

A Purposeful Life

There wasn't much difference between Ralph and Jesse as Olympic runners. Both were superb athletes. Both competed at the top level of their sport. Both were high flyers, and at the 1936 Olympics, the sky was the limit.

Returning home to the "nest" would prove to be another matter entirely. Major achievements, no matter how spectacular, are not permanent. Like anyone else, Jesse and Ralph had to return to their lives and choose what to do next. The choices these two men made led them down very different paths, and the contrast can teach us something about the role of purpose.

We don't know Jesse Owens' purpose for sure, but we do know what the rest of his life looked like. Jesse spent the rest of his life living on Olympic glory. While he accomplished some great things for youth and advancement of athletics, he never quite got past his single victory. From this, we might surmise that Jesse's purpose began and ended with the Olympic Games.

Let's take a look at Ralph's life as a contrast. We do know Ralph stated his purpose was to go to Germany as an Olympian and to serve his country. This sense of purpose manifested itself throughout his life.

After the Olympics, Ralph went back to school and earned a master's degree at USC. He stopped at Xavier next, where he taught and coached track and field. However, Hitler intruded on his life again and so did his purpose. Since serving his country was his calling, he enlisted as a private in 1942. He served in a variety of roles between 1942 and 1945, eventually being decorated and honorably discharged in 1945 as a First Lieutenant.

He returned to Chicago and had a brief but successful business career. However, his purpose called again. It wasn't being fulfilled in business. He became involved in politics in the City of Chicago first, elected as an alderman in 1955. He was elected to the U.S. Congress in 1970.

Take a moment to consider his world at that point. The political machine run by Mayor Richard Daley controlled Chicago. The city struggled with racial tensions, and in 1968 was the scene of several race riots. Those riots pitted the Daley machine against the people of Chicago, mainly from the south and west sides.

Metcalfe was a product of the Daley machine. Elected in 1970, he sought to heal the rifts between the white and black communities, eventually putting himself at odds with the very political machine that elected him. In the process of the fight, he became powerful—so powerful, in fact, he was heralded as the "strongest politician on the south side" in 1976.

In 1978 the Daley political machine decided they had just about enough of Ralph Metcalfe and set out to defeat him. The machine recruited and supported a candidate to run against him in the Democratic primary. It was a hard fought race. The primary race was almost as close as the 100-yard dash in the 1936 Olympics. Only this time Ralph Metcalfe won. It was his turn to break the tape and celebrate. He would have been reelected, but died in October of 1978 before the general election.

After his death, the people he served honored his work and his life purpose. In 1991, a new federal building constructed in Chicago was dedicated to Ralph Metcalfe. Some even say his efforts to heal racial divides in Chicago made possible the election of the city's first African-American mayor, Harold Washington. [4]

Purpose helps you understand where you are going. It keeps you clear, focused, attentive and intentional. It brings you home. With a clear, definite purpose, Congressman Metcalfe learned failure is an event, not a label. He wasn't defined by finishing second, but by fulfilling his purpose. It works the same way for you.

Distraction or Opportunity: How Do You Know?

Distractions often masquerade as opportunities. If we don't have a clear sense of purpose, a firm idea of what's important to us, we tend to run off after every distraction hoping the new and shiny thing will fulfill us and make us happy. For example, let's take a look at Russell.

Russell is a smart guy and by several measures successful. He has had a great career, widely known as the go-to guy in his industry. With his success, he attracts the attention of recruiters. They call him often. Every time they call, he jumps at the chance to talk to another company. As a result, Russell keeps moving. It seems he's always had one eye on the horizon and one foot out the door.

In his current position, those in his industry again see Russell as a successful executive. He made the move with much anticipation after a rigorous interview process. As a member of the senior team, he makes a tangible difference in the culture of the company. He knows most of the 1,000 employees who work for the company and maintains his status as the one member of the senior team who routinely attends employee meetings and special events.

He has relocated with his wife and two kids for every job change. The last move took them near the beach to a great house in a great community. They have fit well into the community and really enjoy their life.

But Russell isn't satisfied. While he has a big impact on the people in his company, he has a nagging sense this isn't the right spot—that the impact isn't broad enough. He doesn't really know what or where the right spot could be, and feels that if he just keeps looking, he will know it when he sees it. However, he also knows where the nagging thoughts can lead. He still gets calls from recruiters, distracting him with their shiny new positions.

Recently, Russell got a call from a recruiter in St. Louis, offering him the opportunity to work for a company with 40,000 employees. In the position, he imagines putting his skills into action would make a significant difference for all 40,000 employees. However, the position would be somewhat insular so his actual impact would be limited.

Russell struggles with the decision. Does he move on or does he stay? Does he stay in a great situation for his family, in a company that is becoming like family? Or does he take a much bigger position in a city that may be seen as less desirable and move his family again?

Remember the cathedral story in the first section of the book? Russell struggles with understanding his reason for working on the cathedral. He doesn't have a clear sense of purpose, or a clear vision of where his life is heading. Without it, everything looks like an opportunity and he will continue yearning for the next thing.

What Would You Say?

Lincoln Financial Group™ is ostensibly a company concerned with the future. You can tell by their TV ads. One series features people's older, future selves who go back in time to give guidance to their younger selves. On the surface, the ads are kind of cheesy. The makeup is pretty bad, and the dialogue is hardly Shakespearean. Even so, there may be a lesson in them about purpose.

Let's look in on one of the ads. A man sits on a plane preparing for takeoff, when out of nowhere an older, grayer version of himself appears in the next seat. He looks over and commends his younger self for saving money by flying coach. After a few comments about the benefits of financial planning (it is an ad, after all), the older self gets up to leave. The younger man asks where he is going, to which his older self replies, "Back to first class; we can afford it now."

What does the ad imply to you about the man's purpose?

In another ad, a woman waits in a hospital hallway, her husband lying in a bed not far away. She is worried, apparently about her husband's precarious health. In this situation she meets her future self. "How's he doing?" the future self asks, as if she doesn't know. She then jumps into a lecture on the benefits of wise investing (perhaps not the best time for a lecture) and then casually says, "By the way, he will be fine."

What possible statements of purpose might you find in this particular instance?

If you had the chance to go back and talk to your younger self, what would you say? Take a moment now to write down three things you would most like to tell a younger you. How would you advise your younger self? What would you tell the child, teenage or young adult you about your purpose?

Defining Your Purpose

While purpose is foundational, we chose to save the discussion of your purpose to the last section of the book. Why? Until now, you may not have been ready to have a discussion about your purpose. You may not have done the work.

Throughout this book you have had the opportunity make some important discoveries about yourself and your life. Have you taken them seriously?

If so, you have a great list of wants, which you prioritized. You developed a vision, articulated your values, and defined your critical success factors. You have developed a number of SMART WAY goals.

Surprise! What you have done is to define your purpose.

You are the one who gets to define your purpose. It doesn't have to be magical, mystical or spoken in hushed, reverential tones. It should be simple, memorable and most of all, yours!

Look over the work you have done. What themes pop out at you? When you defined success and drew your clouds, what cells were the largest? Which ones had the most emphasis?

Now, write your statement of purpose. To do so, fill in the blanks below. Resist the temptation to be too wordy, too conceptual or too concrete.

I live to _____ _____.

Try it on, wear it out and about, and see how the statement resonates in your life. Don't be afraid to massage it, change the words, see how it affects you and the people around you. Does it feel like a fit?

While you're getting comfortable with it, let's take a look how having a defined purpose statement works in the context of living your life.

Focus: Energy Management

Time is Money. We can invest, spend, save, or waste time and money. We manage priorities, energy, choices and tasks. There's no such thing as "time management." You can't "manage" five minutes and get six, nor can you "manage" five dollars and get six. In many ways, time and money are equivalent. Our goals for both are the same:

We do not like to waste time or money. We are disappointed, and sometimes even angry when we feel either of these precious resources has been squandered to no good purpose.

We love to save time and money when we can. In fact, we'll often spend one to save the other, "trading time for money" or "trading money for time" if we feel have more of one than the other to spare. One of the smartest things we can do as professionals is to put an appropriate value on our time and pay others to do things that take time away from money-making activities. Why spend ten hours of your time on bookkeeping or painting when a pro could do a better job in two?

We love to spend time and spend money when we can. Both acts often feel like luxuries. Spending time and money with friends or family is a favorite activity for most of us. Spending time or money on unpleasant obligations is something most of us despise.

The highest and best purpose for both our time and our money is to invest it—to feel we have used it in a way that yields a valuable return.

Time is Not Money. The biggest difference between time and money is that you can get more money. You may gain it, lose it, earn it, spend it or waste it, but one way or another you can get more money. The Federal Reserve literally manufactures more money when it feels the country is running low.

Time, on the other hand, is irreplaceable. Once it's gone, it's gone. Each moment of your life is unique and unrepeatable. Each minute is priceless—the rarest treasure in the universe. By contrast, a dollar is as common as a grain of sand.

So if time is a resource even more precious than money, our best investment strategy for time should involve expert management of the things we can manage: priorities, energy, choices and tasks.

Priorities We've talked about vision, values and mission, and this is where that rubber meets the road. Without those pieces in place, we don't know what our priorities are. We wander from task to distraction to opportunity, tending to address the thing that seems most urgent or most interesting at the moment. At the end of the day, we can't imagine where the time went, and if we ever stop a minute to think, we might wonder or lament about all those lofty dreams from our youth that have never been realized. Our favorite excuse for failure to achieve big things? We're too busy!

Make no mistake: having your priorities straight is unlikely to make you less busy. The difference is when you have clarity, focus, attention and intention, you can devote your time to the things that are really important, rather than just the things that are really shiny.

Energy "Work smarter not harder." I'm sure you've heard (or said) that mantra a thousand times, but how do you translate it into a real strategy? Paying attention to your energy is one way. You already know there are times of day when you seem to be wide awake and others when you're one breath away from collapsing onto your computer keyboard. What do you do with that knowledge?

Each of us has a cycle or a rhythm of energy through each day, with peaks and valleys of mental, physical, and emotional energy. When you know to pay attention to that rhythm, you quickly get a sense of how yours works. Make your plans for the day in harmony with your energy cycles. Need to write a proposal for work? Schedule the task for a time when you have a high level of mental energy. Difficult conversation with your spouse? Not good for those times of day when you tend to be irritable, tired or impatient.

Here's the catch. The best times of day for intense mental work might not be between nine and five Monday through Friday. If you are working a traditional schedule and your body is not cooperating, you may need to look for creative ways to resolve the conflict. Can you shift your work day schedule earlier or later? Work from home one or more days a week? Approach the people who rely on you in your professional role and ask them how you can balance your need for energy management with their need to have access to you.

Choices Dr. Stephen Covey talks about the idea of "integrity in the moment of choice." Even if you know your vision and mission, and you know how to manage your energy, that knowledge does you no good if you don't apply it to your choices. If you know perfectly well you can barely string two coherent thoughts together in the late afternoon, and yet still choose to put off your heavy-duty knowledge work all morning, you haven't exercised integrity in the moment of choice. When this happens, debrief it. You can debrief alone with a journal or by talking into a mirror, or you can talk through it with someone you trust. Ask yourself why you made the choice you did, and review the benefits and the consequences of that choice. Decide whether it was worth it, and what, if anything, you're going to do differently next time.

Every moment of every day is an opportunity to choose well and wisely in service of your vision and mission.

Tasks[5] Once you've sorted out your priorities, gauged your energy and made your choices, it's time to act. By now you've probably figured out that this is all too much to hold in your head, and you're right. Keeping information in your head saps your energy, dulls your wits and destroys your creativity. Suddenly remembering critical appointments or tasks or goals—or being consumed by fear of forgetting them—frustrates and exhausts you, leaving no room for living your life.

Every "eagle" we know has some kind of planning system. It may be as simple as a notebook or as complex as a support staff. It may use the über-geek's dream suite of technological gadgets or nothing but paper and a pen. Your perfect system is as unique as you are. It lets you manage your priorities, energy, choices and tasks in a way that works for you. You'll know it's perfect when you trust it enough to let it hold all your critical information, instead of trying to keep it in your head.

Don't let another moment pass without doing this. Seriously. Put this book down and start assembling a suite of information management tools you find intuitive and inspiring to use and use them. Get rid of anything you don't love or use regardless of what you paid for it. Take the time to consider your personal mechanics—how you best think and work—and build your system carefully and deliberately around your own patterns. You can't write the great American novel, cure cancer or coach football if your pen makes giant inkblots on your notebook and your phone has seventy-two functions which are a mystery to you. Don't waste time fighting with your tools. These are easy things to fix. Get these pointless time-wasters out of your life so you can focus on the stuff that really matters!

To help you in this process, here are some specific questions to consider:

- Which is more valuable to me personally, my time or my money? Why?
- How do my vision and mission translate into daily priorities? How do I record, track, and measure it?
- What are my energy patterns? What, if anything, do I need to change about my day-to-day schedule to take better advantage of them?
- Do I exercise integrity in the moment of choice? Why do I think so or think not? What, if anything, do I want or need to do differently to make better choices?

- Do I have a planning system? Do all the pieces of it work for me? What, if anything, do I need to change, fix, replace or add?

Attention: No Excuses

Have you ever heard the expression, "Fake it until you make it?" You have the ability to create your own success or failure in your head long before you create it in your world. It may start with changing your mind or changing your behavior, but either way, success starts with change. To make something better, you must size up your current circumstances, decide to make a change, then improve and grow. Success comes as a result of improvement and growth, but the process starts with change.

If you want your results to be different in the future, you must first accept that your present situation is not cutting it and you must change in order to improve. Embracing change goes beyond the "decision" to change. You have to experience a change in yourself—a shift in your thinking, your wants, and your willingness to be uncomfortable as you learn something new.

One of the most difficult components of real change is giving up your excuses. Our outward excuses reflect our internal habits of thinking. Our thoughts affect our behaviors. We defend our behaviors with our excuses.

As an example, consider Bill, a retail store owner and a client of Susan's. When he opened his store about a year ago, he never imagined the need he would have for outside sales skills. He thought as long as they opened their doors and provided superior customer service, people would come in droves, checkbooks open and credit cards ready. As you might expect, that wasn't the case. To increase sales, Bill would need to actually go out and sell.

As Bill and Susan explored the world of sales and focused on building his sales skills, he made excuse after excuse for why he couldn't be successful at sales with statements like, "I don't have that bubbly personality needed for networking," "I don't know what questions to ask people so I just don't talk to them," and "I feel bad about interrupting people at work so I can't do cold calls."

We all have our favorite excuses. I'm too busy. I'm too tired. I'm too stressed. I'm too cool. We use everything from the economy to the weather to our shoe size—anything that keeps what we need to accomplish out of our control and beyond our own responsibility. But consider this—when you argue for your excuses, *what do you get when you win?*

When you win the argument in favor of your excuses, you get to stay in your comfort zone, with your old habits of thinking and behaving, comfortably uncomfortable, getting the same results, endlessly recreating your present situation. Those are the benefits, and make no mistake, the benefits are extremely compelling. Raise your hand if you love being uncomfortable. And keep it up there for a couple of days.

Now let's think about the consequences. In Bill's case, they could be devastating. Lack of sales leads to lack of money, which leads to getting behind on the rent and losing the store, defaulting on his business loans, and possibly losing his car or his house since those items are collateral on those loans. All because he made excuses about why he couldn't succeed in sales. Bill failed in his mind before he ever even tried in his actions. Of course, each time he failed in his selling behaviors, this served as "proof" of his belief that he couldn't succeed in sales.

Humans are pattern-matchers. We are brilliant at noticing tendencies and trends. The key is making this pattern-matching gift work for you instead of against you. Sound familiar? Think "affirmations."

Think of something you do regularly, at which you would consider yourself an average performer. It could be anything—cooking, writing, listening, remembering names, estimating figures—but it should be something you would like to be even better at doing. Decide right now that you are great at it. Say it out loud: "I am great at ____."

For the next thirty days, notice consciously when you do that one thing well. Say to yourself, "See? There's the proof I am great at ___." On those rare occasions when your performance is not quite up to snuff, say to yourself, "Huh. That's odd. Normally I'm great at ____." The idea is to catch yourself performing well, in the same way we too often tend to notice only when we perform poorly.

Common knowledge is that humans need at least thirty days to create a new habit. At the end of the thirty days, ask someone else about your performance on this thing you've been fostering. Odds are they'll say you're great at it!

Acting yourself into a new way of thinking is about paying attention to the proof. Be clear about the outcome you want, focus your behavior, and notice every example that supports your intention.

Intention: Commencement

It had been a long week. The business meetings had all gone well, followed by a great golf game and dinner with a customer. Now it was Sunday afternoon and time to go home.

Sitting in his aisle seat, Chip scanned the faces walking down the aisle. Who would take the middle seat? Being a big guy, Chip really hoped for a diminutive seat partner. Someone skinny would be just perfect—someone who wouldn't take up too much space, might provide some pleasant conversation and make it an enjoyable ride home. In the alternative, maybe someone who would keep to themselves so he could catch up on his reading.

No such luck. The guy moving into the seat stood about six foot, three inches, with a big frame and a beard. Both arms were covered in tattoos—brilliant colored ink that covered the visible part of his short sleeve-clad arm. He had ear buds in both ears and he wore some pretty interesting clothing—shorts, a strategically torn T-shirt, and sandals.

When the guy settled in, he took up most of the seat, and he and Chip were closer than two strangers should ever be. The music emanating from his earbuds was hard rock.

When the flight attendant announced it was time to shut down electronic gear, the guy couldn't hear, so Chip poked him. He surprised Chip by offering a pleasant "Hey, thanks, I'm sorry it was so loud." Hmm.

Looking over at the ink covering the guys left arm, Chip noticed the word "PATIENCE" spelled down from the elbow to the wrist. Chip thought perhaps it was the guy's way of reminding himself of his anger management lessons. Curious, Chip asked if the word was tattooed there to remind the guy to be calm and not kill anyone.

"No," replied the guy, "it's the name of my eleven-year-old daughter. She's severely autistic with a chromosomal abnormality that gives her some mild retardation." Chip's breath caught as he took in the jarring contrast to his preconceived notions. Wow, he didn't see that one coming at all. Chip introduced himself and learned "the guy" had a name. Donnie.

"Patience loves The Little Mermaid and she obsesses on the movie." Donnie rolled his wrist to reveal a tattoo of the little mermaid on the inside of his arm. "All the tattoos are creatures or scenes from the movie. You see, I love my daughter," Donnie said. "She's very special to me, and anything I can do to help her live a more normal life, I will do."

Donnie's story isn't unique but it is special. It speaks to the power of preconceived notions as well as the power of intention. Let's face it, you can't show the power of intention or purpose any more than he did than by having both arms tattooed with a daughter's name and favorite cartoon characters.

There are hundreds of Donnies who come in and out of our lives. Lessons are all around us, in the stories told to us and in the stories we tell. Whether we are flying, on the ground or in our nests, we can write the stories of our life in the way we want to.

We invite you to share your stories with us.

JUMP!

As we previously said, an eagle's nest is dozens, if not hundreds, of feet off the ground. So when a baby eagle hatches, grows, and matures, there is exactly one way to leave home. At some moment in a fledgling's life, it has to take a giant leap of faith, literally, and trust its growing wings to hold it up as it takes to the sky.

The same is true with you and your life plan. If you've used our book to start taking an honest look at what you really want, what you value, what you believe, and how you want the rest of your life to play out, you've probably encountered some pretty scary stuff.

Some things about your life may now be very different from how you want them to be, and the prospect of what it's going to take to correct your flight path may fall anywhere between intriguing and terrifying. But if there's one thing we've tried to emphasize through this whole process, it's that change is necessary, inevitable, and when properly planned, *exhilarating*!

As the old saying goes, "If you always do what you always did, you'll always get what you always got." To be sure, change for its own sake is often a waste of energy. But once you have clarity about what you want, focus and attention on how to achieve it, and the intention to do so, there's only one thing left to do: jump out of your nest and SOAR!

End Notes

[1] http://www.merriam-webster.com/dictionary/focus

[2] Chip had the opportunity to hear Captain Haynes tell the story of United Flight 232, and witness the drama first hand. The details of the story recently appeared in *How We Decide,* by Jonah Lehrer, concerning decision making under stress.

[3] *Parade Magazine*, Personality Parade, November 28, 2010

[4] The Ralph Metcalfe story was derived from many sources including Wikipedia (http://en.wikipedia.org/wiki/Ralph_Metcalfe), The Biographical Directory of the United States Congress (http://bioguide.congress.gov/scripts/biodisplay.pl?index=m000675), answers.com (http://www.answers.com/topic/ralph-metcalfe), Black Americans in Congress (http://baic.house.gov/member-profiles/profile.html?intID=62) and others. Suppositions were made from the historical record.

[5] The concepts expressed in the section on "Tasks" are adapted from the work of David Allen in his book *Getting Things Done*. Tracy recommends this book highly as a complement to our book.

Acknowledgments

Chip

When writing a book of this type, many people come to mind to thank. I have really enjoyed the experience with my writing partners. Sue has a warm and giving heart and brings humanity to every story she tells. Tracy keeps us on track, takes care of some of the more detailed issues (em-dash what?) and has an opposing viewpoint on just about everything. The book is so much better than what I could have done by myself. My clients are a big part of my learning, and I enjoy learning from each and every one. One of my best friends is also a client, and I feel blessed he chose to write the foreword for the book. Thanks, Joel. In addition, I have been very fortunate to have many great coaches in my life. Three that come to mind as great sources of learning are David, George and Jerry. Each added to my own personal story, and in fact, it is difficult to know which are my stories and which I have just co-opted, rewritten and made my own. Finally, I would be remiss if I didn't thank Chris, my wife. She has been a great support, believing in me when I absolutely didn't believe in myself. Our story has lasted more than two decades, and I enjoy writing a new page every day.

Acknowledgments

Tracy

It's often said that we teach what we ourselves most need to learn, and I think that's the greatest gift of coaching as a career and of writing a book with brilliant co-authors. I have had an unforgettable experience working with Chip and Sue, and I can't thank them enough for all the ways they have helped and supported me both before and during this project. I also need to thank the coaches who have been so essential in my own growth. Like Chip, I've known many and valued all, and like Chip, I have three in particular I need to mention here: Alan Kovitz, Lee LaPerriere, and Linda Sacha. From the personal side of my life, I must thank my "mirrors": Mike Bakula, Richard Barfuss, and Erik Olson, three people I love and value more than words can express. And lastly, crazy as it may sound to anyone who doesn't know me, I thank Walt Disney, who knew how to dream big and achieve goals better than anybody, and whose magnificent imagination and devotion to quality inspire me every day.

Acknowledgments

Sue

We all have a story (or two) to tell. What we don't often remember is that we also have a story to write, our own life story, which, for me, is a whole lot easier with a little help from my friends. I am honored to have my co-authors, Chip and Tracy, in my corner. In unique and special ways, each teaches, challenges and inspires me to live fully, authentically and on purpose. Like them, I learn from my clients every day, and many of the stories in this book would not be possible without them. A shout out and sincere thank you to the crew from the RAC Knowledge Center (you know who you are) for your gifts of love and laughter, and to the angels at HHT who circle me in light. Special thanks to my coach, Dee Bailey, and to my friends Johan, Alan and Sue, among others, for loving me so much. This project would not be complete without a word of gratitude for my family, my foundation. And finally, thanks be to God for the myriad of gifts he has bestowed. It is my joy to share them with you.

My Personal

Strategic Plan

Strategic Plan
Table of Contents

Purpose

In this section, summarize your purpose in one statement. Answer the following questions:

- How do you define success, both personally and professionally?
- How does it directly apply to what you do or will be doing?
- Who benefits from your success?
- What are your most important wants?
- What do you hope to accomplish in all areas of your life?
- What goals are most important for you to accomplish right now?

Complete your purpose statement, filling in the blanks below:

I live to _____   _____.

Vision Statement

A vision statement has a five to fifteen year horizon and is a description of your quest. It is a verbal painting of what life will look like in the future. It sets forth what you aspire to become, create and achieve. It is how you begin with the end in mind. It is vivid. It is easy to understand and avoids cliches and buzzwords. It inspires action and develops energy.

Vision statements are easiest to remember and have the greatest clarity when they are no longer than twenty words and the shorter the better. Like an affirmation, your vision is best stated in the present, as if you have already achieved it. Here is an example of a vision statement:

"I am the critical link in my family and my relationships. I am judged by the quality of both."

Don't worry if you're not a great wordsmith or if you struggle to come up with the perfect statement, and don't be afraid to keep tweaking it as you gain greater clarity. It's more important to capture the essence of it in a way that makes sense to you, than to have a beautiful sentence, suitable for framing, that doesn't come from your heart. If you need more than twenty words, use them. If your vision is a bulleted list, a song, a poem, a collage of pictures or a slide presentation on your computer and it works for you, great! What matters most is that it is uniquely yours, and it inspires you to live your best life.

Core Values

A key element of a successful planning process is the establishment of no fewer than two and no more than six key values. Throughout your life, you make decisions. Core values lay the foundation for your behavior and decision-making. The values define important truths that guide your actions and those of your employees. They will serve as a guidepost for you as you work to achieve your goals. They provide a framework for your relationship with others and a measure of your congruity.

As you consider your values, consider what you believe to be right. Your values should embody the primary relationships in your life and define how you want them to be carried out. Here are some examples of Core Values:

Integrity: I give my word and keep it. I treat others with uncompromising truth.

Impact: I create positive change in others' lives.

Continuous Learning: I rely on intellectual rigor and I mentor unselfishly.

Trust: I lavish trust on people.

Openness of Thought: I am receptive to new ideas, no matter the source.

Balanced Wellness: I am completely healthy in body, mind and spirit, with a thriving career and deeply satisfying relationships.

Critical Success Factors

Critical Success Factors (CSFs) are those few critical things necessary and sufficient which must happen to achieve what you have defined as success. They must happen in order to accomplish the mission. A CSF will answer the following questions: "What must happen, exist, or be in place to achieve my mission statement? What broad elements are necessary and sufficient to achieve my mission?"

Ideally you should have between three and seven CSFs. More than seven and your focus is scattered. You may find yourself focusing on the trivial rather than the critical. Try to land on just three or four. Here are a few areas you may want to consider as CSFs:

- Investment/Wealth Creation

- Cash Flow

- Social Relationships

- Professional Relationships

- Family Relationships

- Technology

- Education

- Professional Development

- Hobbies

Critical Success Factor:

Goal:		
Action Steps:	**Assigned To:**	**Target Date:**
Time		
Treasure		
Talent		
Manpower		
Machinery		
Providence		
Stupidity		

Critical Success Factor:

Goal:		
Action Steps:	**Assigned To:**	**Target Date:**
Time		
Treasure		
Talent		
Manpower		
Machinery		
Providence		
Stupidity		

Critical Success Factor:

Goal:		
Action Steps:	**Assigned To:**	**Target Date:**
Time		
Treasure		
Talent		
Manpower		
Machinery		
Providence		
Stupidity		

Critical Success Factor:

Goal:		
Action Steps:	**Assigned To:**	**Target Date:**
Time		
Treasure		
Talent		
Manpower		
Machinery		
Providence		
Stupidity		

Tracy Lunquist

Tracy Lunquist has built her life and her business around creating positive change. Her company, Working Magic, offers leadership coaching, instructional design, facilitation and program evaluation. She loves using her creative brilliance to help her clients express theirs.

Many of Tracy's clients are creative people who have found her help invaluable in gaining greater clarity and focus to achieve their goals. Tracy helps her clients notice patterns and set up simple systems to handle life's details so they can invest more energy in pursuing their best ideas.

Tracy holds a Master of Education degree in Human Resource and Organization Development from the University of Illinois at Urbana-Champaign, and has been in business for herself for over ten years. Through work experiences in diverse fields including education, marketing and retail sales, writing has been the common thread.

Samples of Tracy's writing exist everywhere from technical papers to ad copy to executive correspondence. This is the second book project she has completed with coauthors, and looks forward to more team projects and perhaps one or more solo efforts in the future.

Tracy is active in her community, serving a four-year term (2008-2012) as a Commissioner of the West Volusia Hospital Authority as well as maintaining membership in the DeLand Area Chamber of Commerce. She also serves as a chapter officer in the Central Florida Chapter of Women in Aviation, International.

Tracy Lunquist

Working Magic
tracy@workingmagic.net
386-736-5825

Susan Nielsen

Susan Nielsen, President and Founder of Leaderscapes Incorporated,
works with leaders at all levels to help them improve their effectiveness and achieve goals. She is a Certified Business Coach, as well as a speaker, facilitator and author.

Susan is known for creating opportunities for "a-ha moments" with her clients, from the most senior and experienced executives to a clerk on a shop floor. She brings energy, hope, a fresh perspective, and a practical, systems approach to everything she does. Susan understands how organizations work. She blends that knowledge and her understanding of people and behavior to influence positive change.

Susan brings more than 15 years' experience in human relations, recruiting, leadership development, training, and change management. She works primarily with manufacturing companies making the cultural transition to "lean leadership."

Susan holds a Master's degree in Training and Human Resource Development from the University of Wisconsin – Stout, and Bachelor's degrees in English and Mathematics from the University of Wisconsin – River Falls. Susan is a Certified Business Coach, a Certified Professional with the Total Quality Institute, and an active affiliate of Resource Associates Corporation in Reading, PA. She received additional coach training through the Coaches Training Institute (CTI) and is a graduate of CTI's Leadership Program. In 2010, Susan joined St. Mary's University of Minnesota faculty as an Adjunct Instructor in the Organizational Leadership Masters Degree Program.

Susan Nielsen

Leaderscapes Incorporated
susan@leaderscapes.com
651-214-8559

Chip Scholz

Henry E. "Chip" Scholz is Head Coach of Scholz and Associates and is an executive coach, columnist and a public speaker. He works with CEOs, elected leaders, association executives and public and private sector decision makers across North America.

Chip has a straightforward, "tell-it-like-it-is" approach coupled with more than 25 years of management and leadership experience. His clients value him for his insight and ability to cut through the clutter to get to the heart of the issue.

He is a Certified Professional in Behavior, Value and Attribute Analysis, and is a member of Target Training International's Chairman's Club. He is a Certified Business Coach. He has written for ProsCommunications Magazine, 3PL Canada, Greater Charlotte Biz Magazine and other business and trade publications. "The Scholz Report", a monthly newsletter produced and written by Chip, is distributed broadly. Scholz's blog, Leader Snips may be found at www.chipscholz.com. Chip is a co-author of "Masterminds Unleashed: Selling for Geniuses".

Chip currently serves on the board of the International Warehouse Logistics Association in Chicago. He and his wife, Chris, live just outside Charlotte, NC.

Chip Scholz

Scholz and Associates, Inc.
chip@scholzandassociates.com
704-827-4474